The Successful Distance Learning Student

CARL M. WAHLSTROM
Genesee Community College

BRIAN K. WILLIAMS

PETER SHEA
State University of New York

THOMSON
™
WADSWORTH

Australia • Canada • Mexico • Singapore • Spain • United Kingdom • United States

Acquisitions Editor: *Annie Mitchell*
Assistant Editor: *Kirsten Markson*
Technology Project Manager: *Barry Connolly*
Advertising Project Manager: *Linda Yip*
Project Manager, Editorial Production:
 Ritchie Durdin
Print/Media Buyer: *Robert King*
Permissions Editor: *Elizabeth Zuber*

Production Service: *Scratchgravel Publishing
 Services*
Copy Editor: *Carol Lombardi*
Cover Designer: *John Walker Design*
Cover Printer: *Webcom Limited*
Compositor: *Scratchgravel Publishing Services*
Printer: *Webcom Limited*

For more information about our products,
contact us at:

**Thomson Learning Academic
Resource Center**
1-800-423-0563

For permission to use material from
this text, contact us by:

Phone: 1-800-730-2214
Fax: 1-800-730-2215
Web: http://www.thomsonrights.com

Library of Congress Control Number:
 2002108631

ISBN 0-534-57712-1

Wadsworth/Thomson Learning
10 Davis Drive
Belmont, CA 94002-3098
USA

Asia
Thomson Learning
5 Shenton Way #01-01
UIC Building
Singapore 068808

Australia
Nelson Thomson Learning
102 Dodds Street
South Melbourne, Victoria 3205
Australia

Canada
Nelson Thomson Learning
1120 Birchmount Road
Toronto, Ontario M1K 5G4
Canada

Europe/Middle East/Africa
Thomson Learning
High Holborn House
50/51 Bedford Row
London WC1R 4LR
United Kingdom

Latin America
Thomson Learning
Seneca, 53
Colonia Polanco
11560 Mexico D.F.
Mexico

Spain
Paraninfo Thomson Learning
Calle/Magallanes, 25
28015 Madrid, Spain

Contents

Secrets to Success in Distance Learning

You are looking at this book, we assume, because you're a student who has signed up for a distance learning course and you want to know how to excel in it.

It doesn't matter what kind of student you are—college, high school, career military, businessperson, government worker. It doesn't matter what kind of distance learning course you're taking—Internet-based, telecourse, prerecorded video, interactive video, or whatever. Nor does it matter whether the "distance" means you are a wall away or a world away from your instructor. It certainly doesn't matter whether you're full-time or part-time, in a weekend course or a semester course, going for a grade or just for information or training.

What matters is that you realize that distance learning courses are different from traditional classroom courses—so-called "chalk-and-talk" courses—and there are things you need to know to be successful in them. The differences arise, of course, precisely because you and your instructor do not share the same room, and this fact changes the dynamics of the teaching/learning process.

Every book makes a promise to its readers, whether stated or unstated. Here is ours: *If you read this book, we promise that it will help you become not only a successful distance learning student, but a better student in general.*

We realize that you're probably not required to read this book, and that you'd probably like to get through it quickly to glean the most important facts. That's why we've kept it short, only 110 pages of text. Every one of the five short chapters has something for everyone, as follows:

- **Chapter 1, Distance Learning: Education at Your Convenience.** *What it will do for you:* Don't know what the various forms of distance learning are or how likely you are to be successful in a distance learning course? This chapter explains all, in just 19 pages.
- **Chapter 2, Information Technology: The Mind Tools of Cyberspace.** *What it will do for you:* Want to know how the Internet and World Wide Web work, along with e-mail, search engines, and the like? If you're a pro, skip this; otherwise, it's a mini-course in just 24 pages.
- **Chapter 3, Time Management: The Secret to Succeeding at Distance Learning.** *What it will do for you:* Wonder how to handle the seemingly "unstructured" aspects of a distance-course—aspects you may not encounter

in a traditional classroom course? (Actually, many of these you probably will.) These 16 pages may be the most valuable you'll ever read.

- **Chapter 4, Learning Strategies for Distance Learners.** *What it will do for you:* It's one thing to learn to manage your time. Now you need to manage the learning *tasks.* This 32-page chapter explains learning styles; memory techniques; and reading, lecture, and test-taking strategies. Worth its weight in gold. And very applicable to traditional courses, too.
- **Chapter 5, How to Write a Successful Term Paper.** *What it will do for you:* Skip this if no writing is required for your present course. But come back to it when you need a valuable roadmap to the research and writing process. And it's only 19 pages.

Do we deliver on our promise? When you are done reading, we hope that you'll e-mail us and let us know.

Carl Wahlstrom
cmwahlstrom@genesee.edu

Brian K. Williams
briankw1@earthlink.net

Peter Shea
pshea@sln.suny.edu

Distance Learning

CHAPTER

1

Education at Your Convenience

What Is Distance Learning?

Here's a one-paragraph history: In the beginning, there were correspondence schools (sometimes called "matchbook schools" because they advertised on matchbooks). Students signed up for courses in, say, refrigeration repair, and the correspondence school mailed them weekly lessons to be completed and mailed back for grading and credit. Later, in the 1950s, telecourses became available, either on closed-circuit or public-channel television. On their home TV sets, for example, students might watch an instructor on "Sunrise Semester" give an early-morning lecture on history, say, then they would complete written assignments to be mailed in. In the 1970s, computer-assisted instruction came into being, with lessons being given over company computer networks. In the 1990s, the trend toward education via computer networks was given renewed vigor with the widespread popularity of the Internet and World Wide Web.

All these are forms of *distance learning (DL)*, also known as *distance education* and *distributed learning*. The courses are not the "chalk-and-talk" kind, in which you sit in a classroom and an instructor stands in front of a chalkboard and lectures to you. Rather, ___distance learning (DL)___ **is any type of instruction in which student and instructor are not in the same room; they are separated by physical distance.** Thus, you and your instructor might be half a world away from each other or only a classroom wall apart. Instruction might be delivered over the Internet, by television, on prerecorded audiotapes or videotapes, or in print materials that come in the mail.

Who Are You, What Are You Studying, & Why Are You Reading This Book?

While writing this book, we made the following assumptions about you:

WHO YOU ARE   You are a student of any age, full-time or part-time, who is taking a distance learning course, whether it's for a few hours or for an entire semester.

You might be a high school student, a college student, a career-school student, a company employee, a government worker, in the military, or anyone else. You might be in North America, but you could also be anywhere in the world.

WHAT YOU'RE STUDYING   The course you're taking could be in any subject, from English to math to psychology to business to electronics to nursing. Even some courses in art, music, physical education, and medicine are taught by distance learning methods, although DL generally doesn't lend itself to manual skills. (So if you're taking a DL course in swimming, free-hand drawing, band practice, or brain surgery, we hope you'll drop us a line about your experience.)

WHY YOU'RE READING THIS BOOK   You probably picked up this book because you suspect distance learning is somehow different from traditional classroom learning—and you're right. You're hoping to learn some tips and tricks that will help you succeed in this kind of course.

Our purpose is indeed to help you succeed in DL. But you may also find, after reading this book, that the same tips and tricks will help you be a better student in traditional courses as well.

The Two Types of Distance Learning

Basically, distance learning is of two types—*synchronous* and *asynchronous.*

SYNCHRONOUS: AT THE SAME TIME   _Synchronous_ **(pronounced "sin-kren-nuss") means students and instructors are together at the same time.** This, of course, describes the kind of instruction and learning that goes on in a standard chalk-and-talk classroom—instructor and students interact in real time. But this also describes certain types of distance learning. *Examples:* Telephone conferencing, computer conferencing, and interactive television in real time are all forms of synchronous instruction.

ASYNCHRONOUS: NOT AT THE SAME TIME   _Asynchronous_ **("a-sin-kren-nuss") means students and instructors do not need to be together at the same time.** In this situation, you as the student take your lessons anytime, anywhere. The instructor may have presented the lesson minutes or even months before you are exposed to it. *Examples:* Taking a course by mailed correspondence, by the Internet, by audiocassette, or videotape are all forms of asynchronous instruction.

Five Different DL Technologies

Although the old teach-by-mail correspondence schools still exist, this book is principally designed to help students with *technology-based* distance learning. Four kinds of technology are generally used—*telephone, audio, video, computer*—or often a combination of these, called *hybrid*. Instruction may be one way or two way, in delayed time or real time. We consider these in the next five sections.

Telephone

Today the telephone is generally not used as the sole technology for DL instruction, but it's a useful adjunct for helping you keep in touch with the instructor or other students. Communication may be one way or two way; delayed time or real time. Among the uses are the following:

VOICE MAIL   From time to time, you may use ***voice mail* to leave phone messages for others.** (This could include messages left on another person's answering machine or in a voice mail box set up with the phone company.)

FAX   You may use a ***fax machine* to transmit copies of print or graphic materials** over telephone lines.

AUDIOCONFERENCING   On occasion, you may do ***audioconferencing*, wherein you and others in different locations have a telephone conference in real time** to exchange views. Audioconferencing (you can have a telephone operator set up a conference call for you) may be useful when several people are trying to come to an agreement about how to proceed on a joint project, for example.

Audio

"Audio" means delivering learning materials to the ear alone. Most likely this would mean you receive audiotapes to play in an audiotape player or audio CDs to play in a CD player or on a personal computer. All such instruction is one way, delayed time. For example, you can get a series of tapes to listen to in your car on such subjects as conversational French or the history of jazz. (In addition, it's possible to receive distance learning instruction via radio. And you could hear sound files stored on the Internet, as we'll discuss in Chapter 2.)

Video

"Video" means using television as a learning medium. Video instruction takes the following forms:

VIDEOTAPES: ONE WAY, DELAYED TIME   Documentaries and feature films are often available on ***videotapes*, which can be played on a videocassette recorder (VCR).** You may already have seen these in live classroom situations—in traffic school, an instructor may show you the effect of car impacts on crash dummies, for instance. They are equally useful for distance learning.

For instance, certain courses, such as Principles of Economics, are available as a series of videotapes. Or you might obtain a documentary on a videocassette tape from your school's library for viewing at home. Or you might download a video on your home computer. Often videotaped courses are accompanied by a textbook and study guide that you work through.

TELECOURSES: ONE WAY, DELAYED TIME OR REAL TIME   _**Tele-courses**_ **are television programs, either prepackaged or real time, that are carried over cable or public broadcasting channels.** The agency making the telecourse available will usually mail you a study guide that provides directions and homework assignments.

You may receive the instruction over a television monitor in a classroom. Or you may view it at home on your TV or, if your PC is properly equipped, on your computer screen.

INTERACTIVE VIDEO: TWO WAY, REAL TIME   _**Interactive video**_ **is televised instruction in which instructors can give lessons and can have a discussion with students in real time.** _Interactive_ means "back and forth," as when you're having a conversation or are playing a video game.

The instructor gives his or her lecture from a location equipped with television camera, microphone, and possibly TV monitor and sound system. The students are in one or more other locations, and they can communicate with the instructor by telephone.

Or, if both instructor and students are set up for _**videoconferencing**_—**that is, linked by both voice and video—they may take turns having a conversation either way.** In videoconferencing, students are in interactive visual communications (IVC) classrooms or conference rooms, which are equipped with TV sets, speakers, cameras, and microphones for two-way communication between the instructor and students.

Computer

The widespread availability of the personal computer and access to the Internet has led to all kinds of learning possibilities.

CD-ROM/DVD OR FLOPPY DISK ON STAND-ALONE COMPUTER: ONE WAY, DELAYED TIME   Just as lessons can be delivered by videotape, they can also be delivered by _**floppy**_, _**CD-ROM**_, or _**DVD disks**_, **which are media for storing information from a computer.** As a student, you would insert the disk into the floppy-disk drive or CD-ROM/DVD drive in your personal computer and view the material on your screen.

Unlike videotapes, however, this kind of material is apt to be _interactive_, allowing you to proceed through the lessons at your own pace. With this form of instruction, you can use a stand-alone computer; it need not be linked to the Internet.

NETWORK-BASED INSTRUCTION: ONE WAY, DELAYED TIME   You can receive instruction one-way over some form of computer _**network**_—**a system of interconnected computers, cell phones, or other communications de-**

vices that can communicate with one another. A number of variations and services are available with networks:

- **Types of networks:** A network could be a **_local area network (LAN)_, a small network that connects computers and devices in a limited geographical area,** such as one office or a group of buildings on a college campus. Or it might be a **_wide-area network (WAN)_, which covers a wide geographical area such as a country or the world,** using satellites, fiber-optic cable, and a variety of other connections.

   The greatest WAN, of course, is the **_Internet_, the worldwide network that connects up to 400,000 smaller networks in more than 200 countries.**

- **E-mail:** An instructor might transmit homework instructions to students via **_e-mail_—"electronic mail"—which consists of text messages transmitted over a computer network.**

- **The World Wide Web:** Students might be asked to visit a lesson on a site on the **_World Wide Web_ (the "Web")—a worldwide system of interconnected computers that store information not only in text form but also as still images, moving images, and sound.**

   The Web is different from the Internet in that the Web offers information as *multimedia*—that is, "multiple media," which include not only text but also animation, streaming audio, and streaming video, as we discuss in Chapter 2. You access the Web by using a **_Web browser_, a kind of software that enables you to read electronic documents.** The most well-known browsers are Microsoft Internet Explorer and Netscape Navigator, although others are available, such as Opera. (If you're not familiar with the Internet, the World Wide Web, browsers, and so forth, we discuss these subjects further in Chapter 2.)

   In the above three network arrangements, instruction is a one-way street: The instructor instructs and the student learns; there is no back-and-forth interaction. In addition, this form of DL is usually asynchronous—the student usually gets information in delayed form, not in real time.

NETWORK-BASED INSTRUCTION: TWO WAY, DELAYED TIME   One of the great features of networks (including the Internet) is that they are not necessarily a one-way street. You as a student might e-mail your instructor a question in the morning, and the instructor might e-mail a response in the afternoon—an example of delayed-time (asynchronous) interaction.

Some other types of delayed-time network interaction are as follows:

- **E-mail:** You and your distance learning classmates might e-mail each other, as when working on a class project, all of you responding to each others' messages in delayed time as your schedules permit.

- **Listservs:** You might also join a **_listserv_, an e-mail mailing list that allows the sending of messages to many individuals simultaneously and enables multiple users to engage in continuing discussion,** sending messages as their time permits. You become a subscriber to a listserv by sending an e-mail to the listserv moderator requesting that you be put on the mailing list.

- **Web bulletin boards:** A variant on the delayed-time discussion forum is the **_bulletin board_ or _threaded discussion group_, in which people with the same interest communicate with each other by sending messages to the same Website.** For instance, you might contact all your classmates at once by sending ("posting") just one message to the class bulletin board set up by your instructor.

- **Newsgroups: _Newsgroup_ is the name given to a discussion forum on Usenet, a network of thousands of such groups accessible with certain Internet connections.** We expand on this in Chapter 2.

- **Asynchronous course management systems: _Course management systems_ are off-the-shelf solutions for organizing online learning in a way that is easier for learners, teachers, and administrators**. Examples of CMS packages are Blackboard, WebCT, Prometheus, and ANGEL. These programs combine all the functions listed above (and some synchronous functions) into a single-course Website that is protected by a password.

NETWORK-BASED INSTRUCTION/COMPUTER CONFERENCING: TWO WAY, REAL TIME   Networks, and the Internet in particular, also allow distance learning students to communicate with each other in real time (that is, synchronous communication).

Three methods are as follows:

- **Chat rooms: A _chat room_ is an online space in which participants have simultaneous discussions by typing messages on their computers; the messages appear instantaneously on participants' screens.** IRC, MUD, and MOO are technologies enabling people to "chat" or communicate in real time with each other.

    An *IRC*, for *Internet relay chat*, is a section of the Internet in which users can communicate with others by typing messages that immediately appear on the screens of other users.

    A *MUD*, for *multi-user dungeon* (or *domain*), is a text-only computer network program to which users can connect so that they can communicate in real time about common issues. Because the term grew out of the "virtual reality" game of Dungeons and Dragons (which was developed for multi-users on the Internet), educators prefer to use the name *MUV*, for *multi-user virtual environment*, to reduce its association with sometimes-violent online games.

    In a *MOO* (for *multi-user object-oriented environment*), users can also exchange messages in real time; it differs from a MUD in that it incorporates pictures. As a user, you would take on the appearance of a computerized character (an avatar), which enables you to walk around and chat with other characters (or students).

- **Desktop videoconferencing: _Desktop videoconferencing_ allows people with camera- and microphone-equipped personal computers to communicate with one another in real time.** Technologies such as CUSeeMe provide the necessary software plus a small camera that sits atop the user's computer monitor. The viewer sees the other person in a small window on the computer screen. The software not only allows users to see others at the same time but also to simultaneously share and work on documents.

A difficulty with videoconferencing by computer is that images on the screen may not flow as smoothly as those on television. That is, because of the slowness of the delivery system (a result of inadequate bandwidth), people's movements may seem a bit jerky and out of sync with the speakers' voices.

- **Whiteboards: An electronic _whiteboard_ is a computer program that allows users to draw on their display screen and share the information with other participants on the network.** The software (similar to Windows Paint) allows you not only to do some freehand drawing but also to use lines, arrows, triangles, and other shapes. Usually whiteboards are used while the participants simultaneously do audioconferencing or e-mail each other.

Hybrids

Today many distance learning courses take place on **_hybrid technologies_, which combine various technologies for communicating via networks.** For example, you might receive much of your instructional materials and homework on a Website, but you would return your assignments to the instructor via e-mail and you might meet with your fellow students in some sort of forum that combines audioconferencing and even whiteboards. _Hybrid_ may also include the practice of combining online technologies with traditional classroom teaching.

ADVANTAGES & DISADVANTAGES OF DISTANCE LEARNING

You probably came to your distance learning course with certain expectations about its advantages and probably even its disadvantages. Let's see how your expectations check out:

ADVANTAGES   Here are some of the advantages of a DL course compared to a traditional classroom course.

- **_Flexibility:_** Clearly the greatest rationale for the existence of most forms of DL is that students can do much of the work at times and places of their choosing. For example, students can take online courses after work hours. Military personnel can take courses from all over the world. Parents with small children can finish getting a degree. Traveling businesspeople can complete courses while on the road.

  Flexibility is not always the case, of course, with certain forms of synchronous instruction. With live telecourses, for example, students have to show up at an appointed time at a particular video-equipped classroom. Even telecourses, however, give instructors more flexibility in that they can teach more students than would be possible with a single classroom.

- **_Self-tailored learning:_** Within certain limits, distance learning may allow students to learn at their own pace, in their preferred medium, or in a more comfortable environment. Students may log on and off at will, so they can read at times of their own choosing instead of trying to keep up with the teacher. A hearing-impaired student might be able to learn better from a print-based Internet class than from a traditional classroom. Shy students may find themselves better able to participate in class discussion in an online course than in a regular classroom.

- **More choices:** Even students taking traditional classes have discovered the benefits of distance learning. *Example:* College students enrolled in regular classes often find they can't get required courses because the courses are full or there is a schedule conflict. DL may allow them more choices in course offerings and times.
- **More personal attention:** Some students in Internet-based courses find they actually get more individual attention from their instructor than they would in a conventional course.

DISADVANTAGES   You need to be aware that there are certain disadvantages to DL.

- **Importance of self-discipline and time management:** The most significant disadvantage (and the reason we wrote this book) is: DISTANCE LEARNING REQUIRES MORE SELF-DISCIPLINE AND TIME MANAGEMENT. When students drop out of a distance learning course, they often tell us it's because they lost their grip on time management. They say they missed the external discipline of being required to show up for a class. Later in this chapter we address the matter of personal motivation in "The Discipline of Distance Learning," p. 18. In Chapter 3 we give you tips for better time management.
- **Possible expense:** For some people, another disadvantage may be the expenditures required for, say, computer equipment and Internet hookups. Of course, these must be weighed against the usual expenses of taking a conventional course, such as commuting, parking, and perhaps babysitting.
- **Possible loneliness:** Yet another disadvantage may be simple loneliness. Some students feel lonely without face-to-face contact with other students, no matter how much they may communicate with others by phone or e-mail.
- **More reading and writing:** Internet-based distance learning courses in particular rely less on lectures as a means of instruction and more on reading and discussion. Thus, students who are uncomfortable with their reading and writing skills may find themselves equally uncomfortable with their DL course.

THE ENVIRONMENT OF DISTANCE LEARNING: TECHNOLOGY & THE LEARNING PROCESS

With most kinds of asynchronous instruction—receiving DL lessons via printed material, audiotapes, videotapes, or CD-ROMs—your study environment and habits won't be appreciably different from what you're used to doing as plain old homework for traditional classes. You'll read and reread or play and replay the material until you think you've learned it. (We present secrets of learning and memorization in Chapter 4.)

With live telecourses and with some computer videoconferencing, the skills required may be much the same as those you use in a regular lecture classroom. (Chapter 4 also contains tips on taking lecture notes.)

What's different about so much of distance learning, however, is *the reliance on the Internet as a mechanism for advancing learning.* And use of the Internet quite definitely gives the whole learning experience a far different feel from what you may have been accustomed to. In a nutshell, compared with traditional classroom courses, MOST INTERNET-BASED COURSES EMPHASIZE COMMUNICATION AND COLLABORATION, BOTH WITH THE INSTRUCTOR AND WITH FELLOW STUDENTS.

Let us describe what this environment might be like.

Getting Started

We are assuming that you have discovered how to enroll in a distance learning class and paid the necessary fees, if any. We'll also assume you have the textbooks and other course materials, as well as the necessary computer equipment and Internet connection. (Read Chapter 2 if you think you need additional background about using the Internet and World Wide Web.) Finally, we'll assume that you have already been sent a packet of materials about the course.

It may be that you will mainly rely on your e-mail software and your Web browser for communicating in this course. On the other hand, you may be required to have collaboration software (such as NetMeeting, Symposium, or CUSeeMe) so that you can meet others online, communicate through both text and audio, and view images together. Or you may participate in predesigned programs (offered by such services as Blackboard, edCenter, ed2go.com, or WebCT) that offer clear instructions for users. Such matters will be explained in the course information packet.

Incidentally, if you have an opportunity to obtain some sort of orientation to the technology you'll be using—which many schools offer either online or on campus—we strongly advise taking it, because it will make your DL efforts much easier.

The Course Packet or Syllabus

What is in the course information packet? If the course is for credit, as for a college subject, it should contain a **_syllabus_ (pronounced "_sill_-uh-buss"), a course guide that tells you readings to cover, test dates, and due dates for papers or projects.**

THE SYLLABUS IS VERY IMPORTANT BECAUSE IT SUMMARIZES YOUR GAME PLAN FOR THE COURSE. The syllabus is important in any course, whether DL or not, because it gives you the road map for success in the course. You should give the syllabus the attention it deserves, because it clearly identifies due dates, the nature and scope of the assignments, and other important parameters of the class (for instance, test make-up procedures, acceptable formats for papers, and so on).

This kind of information is standard with regular chalk-and-talk courses. The distance learning packet, however, should also include such information as

- How to contact the instructor
- The Web address for the course's home page, if applicable
- How you're expected to interact with the instructor and other students
- A course overview
- Learning objectives
- Readings (both online and "off line"—that is, in traditional texts)
- Course schedule, with dates for quizzes, tests, papers, and the like
- How learning will be evaluated or graded
- Perhaps some information on supportive student services, if available

Exams, Tests, & Quizzes

No doubt one of the first questions that comes to mind is "How do they test you in this course?" You may ask, "What protection do they have against people cheating—especially if students are working on computers from home?"

There are five different possibilities discussed below.

NO TESTS AT ALL   It's possible the course will have no tests at all—no quizzes, no midterms, no final exams. This is particularly apt to be true if the course you're taking is for training purposes—for example, a company's in-house course about how to treat customers better or repair new equipment.

However, even some for-credit courses may not require testing. Instead, your course grade may be based on other things—the papers you submit, the presentations you make, your responses on problem-solving assignments, the extent of your interaction in class chat-room/threaded discussion, how well you and your fellow students perform on a collaborative class project, and so on.

ONLINE OPEN-BOOK TESTS   In an ***open-book test*, test-takers are allowed to answer questions with their textbooks and other learning materials readily available.** In an online course, the student might be given a time limit to take an open-book test while sitting at the same home computer over which he or she has been taking the course throughout the term.

Open-book testing makes the learning materials accessible to all, but the students who have been keeping up in the course will have the advantage because they will know how to quickly find and organize the material for their answers.

PROCTORED TESTS AT THE SCHOOL'S LOCATION   A ***proctor* is a person appointed to supervise students at an examination.** The proctor may be the course instructor or it might be, say, a graduate student. The proctor checks students' identification to prevent someone else from taking the test in a student's place. Then the proctor must watch students during the test-taking period to make sure they are not using illegal help (such as notes hidden under the visor of a baseball cap or hand signals from fellow students).

With some distance learners, the school may require students to go to the school's main campus on a given day for the purpose of taking a proctored test. Of course, this method can be an inconvenience for students who must take time off from work or drive a long distance to the campus.

PROCTORED TESTS AT A REMOTE LOCATION   In another method of proctoring, a student is allowed to take a test in a remote location, but the proctor is someone that the instructor trusts to do an honorable job of monitoring. Some colleges, for example, have extension centers or satellite campuses, and students go there to take exams. If you are a U.S. serviceperson stationed at a military base in Germany but taking a DL course originating in California, you might take a proctored exam under the watchful eye of the base chaplain, the post librarian, or a professor at a nearby German university. Or if you live in Idaho but are taking a DL class originating in Texas, you might arrange to take the test at a local university or high school. The proctor needs to be identified and approved by your DL instructor.

ONLINE TESTS—PASSWORD-PROTECTED   A *password* **is a special word, code, or symbol required to access a computer system.** No doubt you will be required to have a password in order to access any Internet part of your distance learning course to begin with. That same password is what, instructors hope, will guarantee the integrity of the work being submitted to them online by a student in their DL class.

Some online quizzes may be automatically scored in order to give students detailed feedback. Some tests even simulate laboratory experiments, as in physics, so that you can manipulate scientific data to test a hypothesis.

ONLINE TESTS—HONOR SYSTEM   There's probably no infallible way to ensure that any online work being submitted is the product of the actual enrolled student. Even a password and security system can't guarantee that the online student taking the test is the only one in the room. (To be sure, however, DL courses using televised computer conferencing systems, or webcams, make it harder for this kind of illegal assistance to take place.)

Thus, many online courses are run on the *honor system*—**that is, students are on their honor not to cheat and instructors do not check that students are other than who they say they are.** In such cases, much of the evaluation or grading may rest on other work produced besides test results, such as collaborative projects, reaction papers, and term papers.

Term Papers & Class Projects

If you're in a for-credit course, you'll probably be required to write a term paper, just as you would in a traditional course. (We describe how to organize, research, and write successful papers in Chapter 5.)

Class projects may be used more frequently in DL courses than they are in traditional face-to-face courses. Sometimes the reason is that instructors are able to assign a grade to the project rather than having to evaluate an individual student's contribution to a collaborative project. In a DL sociology course, for example, students might be asked to collaborate on developing a research problem that follows the steps in the scientific method. If the project receives an "A," then all the contributors to it each get an "A." Of course, it's up to the participating students to deal with any slackers—perhaps by registering a complaint with the instructor. In effect, then, group social pressure is used to make sure each participant contributes fairly to the group result. However, many instructors avoid giving out group grades unless they are able to determine (perhaps through individual quizzes or papers) that they are absolutely fair to all members.

Labs

How are you going to handle those parts of a course that require hands-on experience, as is usual with chemistry, teaching, nursing, and the like? **_Laboratories_ are courses or parts of courses designed to allow experimental study in a science or other discipline.** Biology courses have biology labs, in which students may look at specimens under a microscope. Language courses have language labs, in which students may practice their pronunciation and recognition skills.

Usually what happens is that traditional on-campus students will take the theory or principles part of a course online because it's offered at convenient hours or otherwise suits their schedules. But then they take the lab component of such a course in the traditional way—by going to a site where they can pour the chemicals, observe the children, or whatever. In other words, there is no online component for the lab.

True distance learning students who have to deal with a lab or internship requirement have to make other arrangements. For instance, they may spend a couple of Saturdays a month attending all-day labs on campus. Or perhaps they can use the facilities of a local high school. Or they may receive a lab kit from their instructor. Finally, some DL courses offer online labs that simulate experiments, much as a novice pilot might train on an aircraft simulator.

THE EXPERIENCE OF SYNCHRONOUS LEARNING

Students in traditional classroom courses are used to instructors who stand in front of a class and lecture. This experience can be duplicated, of course, with telecourses or with computer videoconferencing. As in regular lecture classes, you need to present yourself at a certain location—a classroom using two-way video or a computer using conferencing software—at regular times, such as the same hour three times a week.

In addition, students attending traditional classes are accustomed to a fair amount of interaction with their instructors and other students. These experiences too can take place with synchronous forms of instruction, including use of online chat rooms.

As an additional feature, synchronous distance learning allows for multiple instructors to teach the same class, either simultaneously or sequentially. Thus, for example, three instructors might team-teach (at successive sessions) a social studies class on the subject of terrorism: one from a history department, another from a branch of the government, a third from a specialized "think tank."

As mentioned above, however, more and more distance learning classes are apt to use a combination or hybrid of technologies. Thus, for example, you might find that the bulk of your in-class experience is a lecture in real time, delivered live in a traditional classroom or synchronously through a telecourse or computer-conferencing arrangement. But the rest of your course experience might be asynchronous: You engage in discussion and projects with your classmates and submit assignments through e-mail and Websites.

THE EXPERIENCE OF ASYNCHRONOUS LEARNING

Let's consider how instructional materials are presented in asynchronous learning and how assignments are covered, mainly through use of the Internet. By and large, we think you'll find these are not much different from what many students are used to, although the details and the means are different.

DELIVERY OF CORE MATERIAL: TAPE, CD-ROM, OR INTERNET?
Every course consists of core material, the main principles and facts that you are expected to master. In the usual live classroom format, this material is delivered in the instructor's lecture and is augmented by the textbook and other readings. In asynchronous DL, this core material may be presented as prepackaged lectures on audiotapes, videotapes, or CD-ROMs/DVDs.

In Internet-based courses, core material may also be presented in the form of lectures, as in e-mail text form, Web-page form, or real-time computer video-conferencing form. More and more often, however, instructors in such courses are not presenting lectures at all. Instead, students are expected to rely on the textbook, other readings, instructor questions, and class discussion and projects to learn the core material. (Incidentally, a good online course will feature a helpdesk to help you through technical difficulties.)

THE USE OF THE COURSE WEBSITE TO MOVE THE COURSE ALONG The course Website provides the touchstone for the course. The instructor may use it to introduce various parts of the course throughout the term, providing students with new reading assignments, quizzes, self-tests, projects, and discussion topics from time to time.

After students complete the assignments, they will submit them to the instructor in any of the ways agreed upon: by regular mail, by e-mail, by posting to the Website, or whatever (usually specified in the syllabus).

THE USE OF ONLINE DISCUSSION GROUPS: MAKE SURE YOU SHOW UP Discussion groups may be a big part of a DL course. Here you are expected to log onto (connect to) the class chat room, threaded discussion, or other forum according to the schedule set by the instructor. You should then actively participate in and initiate discussion. If the instructor designates you to lead discussion, you should do so. You should always communicate in a respectful and courteous way.

Some instructors may use the first discussion group as a "getting to know you" forum. Students may be asked to introduce themselves and to share background information—in some cases, even to exchange photographs (by posting digital pictures) of themselves.

In asynchronous discussion groups, of course, there will be a lag time between responses, as students check in at times of their convenience. Still, students need to be aware that it's important to return to each online discussion forum in a timely fashion—otherwise there is no discussion.

COMMUNICATING WITH THE INSTRUCTOR: GETTING FEEDBACK AND ANSWERS TO QUESTIONS   The teacher–student interaction is one of the unique and positive aspects of distance learning. Indeed, some students find that DL actually provides *more* interaction with the instructor than occurs in regular courses. Instructors themselves say that the feedback and interaction are the keys to making distance learning effective.

What can you expect from your instructor? When you submit an assignment, you should expect to receive comments back. This may come in the form of, say, e-mail messages or as annotations on e-mail attachments. When you ask your instructor a question—whether by letter, voice mail, e-mail, or query to a Website—you should expect a response. Of course, if you are not communicating during the time the instructor has indicated to be his or her office hours or availability, you'll need to allow for the delayed response.

THE BEST WAY TO MAKE A GOOD IMPRESSION ON THE INSTRUCTOR, incidentally, is to turn in your assignments on time and to avoid showing off by submitting a lot of "extra stuff" to try to impress the instructor with your special knowledge. The reason we say this is that teaching an online course is actually more time-consuming for the instructor than teaching a traditional course. This is because of all the additional interaction required. (After all, think how long it takes to *write* a response to a student question than to *speak* that response.) Some instructors, for instance, may average 40 or 50 e-mails a day for a single course. These instructors do not, therefore, appreciate receiving pages of material copied from the Internet.

COMMUNICATING WITH YOUR CLASSMATES: SHARING AND WORKING TOGETHER   As we mentioned, distance learning courses, particularly those structured around the Internet, tend to seek alternatives to the lecture format. This means you will probably be doing a lot more communicating with your classmates—more than you would in a traditional class.

This makes distance learning an unusually enriching experience. Many of your fellow students may be quite different from ordinary or traditional students: working students, parents, overseas students, and so on.

Some of the sharing and working you will do with other students may come in the form of collaborative projects assigned by the instructor. Other interaction will be in mandated discussion groups. You may also want to join forces with others in informal study groups, whether via chat room, videoconferencing, or even in face-to-face meetings. Finally, you may feel you need to interact with other students in order to get additional help, to download (retrieve from the Internet) a file of materials you don't have, or to catch up on assignments.

How Will You Fare as a Distance Learner?

You've probably spent a good deal of your life exposed to traditional forms of teaching. That is, you sit in a classroom, and an instructor in front of a blackboard teaches you through lectures and class discussion.

Although distance learning can resemble the traditional classroom format (as in live broadcast telecourses), much of the instructor–student interaction can be quite different, as we've described so far. How are you going to fare in this new environment?

Consider the usual live lecture class in high school or college. It often has the same daily or weekly schedule, and you're expected to show up for class (the instructor may even take attendance). Such classes are *structured environments*. Distance learning classes, by contrast, can be highly *unstructured environments*. Although it's possible you'll be required to show up at the same instructional site on a regular basis, it's also likely you'll have a lot more choice about it. The chief characteristic of distance learning, therefore, is that it offers more convenience. This means that YOU'LL HAVE MORE FREEDOM, BUT YOU'LL ALSO HAVE MORE RESPONSIBILITY.

IDENTIFYING YOUR CONCERNS ABOUT DISTANCE LEARNING   A certain amount of anxiety can actually motivate you to accomplish positive results. Anxiety about losing a game (or the will to win) makes you alert, focuses the mind, and induces you to try to do well. Similarly, some fear of losing the game of learning can motivate you to do your best. Too much anxiety, however, can motivate you to perform negatively. That is, you may be so overwhelmed by fear that you want to withdraw from the competition. This can and does happen to some students. But it need not happen to you.

It's important to identify your concerns and fears about distance learning so you can take steps to deal with them. Take a few minutes to try the Self-Analysis quiz in the box on the following page.

COMMON FEARS OF DISTANCE LEARNING STUDENTS   The following fears are common to many college students, but they apply to distance learning students as well.

- Fear of flunking—this may be the biggest.
- Fear of not being able to manage everything.
- Fear of the pressure—of the work and responsibility, of not being able to compete.
- Fear of technology.
- Fear of loneliness, of not finding supportive friends.

Self-Analysis: What Are Your Fears About Distance Learning?

Identifying your fears is the first step in fighting them. For each of the following statements, circle the number below corresponding to how much you agree or disagree: 1 = strongly disagree; 2 = somewhat disagree; 3 = neither disagree nor agree; 4 = somewhat agree; 5 = strongly agree.

I am afraid that . . .

1. This class will be too difficult for me.	1 2 3 4 5
2. I will miss the fellowship of a live class.	1 2 3 4 5
3. I might flunk.	1 2 3 4 5
4. I won't be able to handle the amount of work required.	1 2 3 4 5
5. My study habits won't be good enough to succeed.	1 2 3 4 5
6. I'll won't be able to handle the technology.	1 2 3 4 5
7. I'll be a disappointment to people important to me, such as my parents, family, or children.	1 2 3 4 5
8. I won't have enough time and will have to drop out.	1 2 3 4 5
9. I won't be able to handle working and/or family responsibilities and the class at the same time.	1 2 3 4 5
10. I will get depressed.	1 2 3 4 5
11. I won't be able to manage my time being on my own.	1 2 3 4 5
12. I'll oversleep or otherwise won't be able to participate.	1 2 3 4 5
13. I won't be able to maintain the grade average I want.	1 2 3 4 5
14. The instructor will find out that I'm basically incompetent and will kick me out.	1 2 3 4 5
15. I won't be able to compete with other students.	1 2 3 4 5
16. I won't make any friends.	1 2 3 4 5
17. I won't be able to overcome my shyness.	1 2 3 4 5
18. I'll have problems with my family/housemates.	1 2 3 4 5
19. I won't be able to handle writing/spelling or math.	1 2 3 4 5
20. My instructor will think I'm a dope.	1 2 3 4 5

(continued)

- Fear of not finding one's way around.
- Fear of running out of money and having to drop out.

Many students express concerns about not being able to balance their schoolwork and their family and/or job responsibilities.

WHY DO SOME PEOPLE HAVE TROUBLE WITH SCHOOL?   Aside from lack of money, people who end up dropping usually do so for the following reasons:

- **They are underprepared academically, which leads to frustration.** Some students are underprepared—in reading, writing, and math skills, for instance—and find themselves in courses that are too difficult for them. (Then they may be angry and resentful because they think someone has

(continued)

21. There will be no one to help me.	1 2 3 4 5
22. I'll choose the wrong topics for a paper or discussion.	1 2 3 4 5
23. I'll have to cheat in order to survive the tough academic environment.	1 2 3 4 5
24. My family or my job will complicate things, and I won't be able to keep up.	1 2 3 4 5
25. Other (write in):	1 2 3 4 5

_____

_____

Add the number of points: _____

Meaning of Your Score

100–125: High   You are very fearful or very concerned about your distance learning experience. Although these concerns are not unusual, it would be a good idea to check into some school or institutional resources to assist you in dealing with your worries. Such resources include computer lab staff, career and personal counseling, the school's learning center, and the financial aid office.

75–99: Average   You are somewhat fearful or somewhat concerned about your distance learning experience. Welcome! Join the crowd! Your concerns are typical and are shared by the majority of students. Although you'll probably do just fine, you could check out the resources described above.

74 or less: Low   You have few fears, perhaps are even laid back about this new experience. (Don't think it's going to be a piece of cake, however.)

Interpretation   We all tend to think that any one worry we have is unique, that it is ours alone, and that no one else ever experiences it with the intensity that we do. This is not true! Indeed, the fears and concerns listed above are quite common. So is the reluctance to seek help, to get support. But seeking support is probably what will help you overcome the fear.

somehow set them up.) *It's important to know that many schools offer all kinds of academic support services—for example, math tutoring. But it's best not to wait until you're in trouble to find them.* Many schools are developing online tutoring for a variety of courses.

If you sense, even in the first couple of weeks of your first term, that you're slipping, we recommend telling the instructor of the class for which you are reading this book. Or, if you can, go to a student counseling center, if one is available. Be honest also about telling those who have some influence on your program if you're worried about being in over your head.

- **They are overprepared academically, which leads to boredom.** Some students complain that their courses repeat work they already covered elsewhere, perhaps in high school. This is why good advising by a counselor is important.

- **They perceive the course as being not useful.** Students who don't think their schoolwork will be useful beyond the classroom can be strong candidates for dropping out. It's important, then, to nail down the reasons why you're taking the class. You also need to appreciate the concept of ***deferred gratification*—postponing immediate pleasures in the belief that the class will lead to even greater benefits later.**
- **They have unrealistic expectations.** Some students don't have realistic expectations about themselves and distance learning. For example, some expect great things to happen without much investment on their part. Thus, they devote little effort to making distance education work for them.
- **They don't have a personal support system.** Even on-campus students have to start from scratch to build a personal support system. This means making friends with other students, counselors, and instructors or otherwise finding support. Often distance learning students are isolated to begin with. Thus, we hope you have a support system in your family and friends.

In general, all these difficulties can be boiled down to three matters: (1) motivation, (2) support, and (3) skills achievement. We hope that with the help of this book, you can get beyond your fears and make distance learning the success you want it to be.

THE IMPORTANCE OF STAYING POWER   If more is required of you in distance learning than in regular courses, what is going to pull you through? One important secret to success is developing STAYING POWER—*perseverance* or *persistence.* "Nothing takes the place of persistence," President Calvin Coolidge stated. "Talent will not. Nothing is more common than unsuccessful people with talent. Genius will not. Unrewarded genius is almost a proverb. Education will not. The world is full of educated derelicts. Persistence alone has solved and always will solve the problems of the human race."

The importance of your ability to stay the course, to persevere, to hang on with the going gets tough, cannot be underestimated. If you had or have obstacles to overcome—for instance, you didn't have a good high school experience or you have to juggle a job and children along with going to school—you can still be successful. In fact, you will find that similar circumstances or hardships apply to many students. Yet they still manage to get through school.

THE DISCIPLINE OF DISTANCE LEARNING: THE KEY IS SELF-MANAGEMENT

Now that you have a rough idea of what distance learning entails, as well as an understanding of your own concerns about it, it's time to consider what it takes to make a success in this kind of course. Here are some questions to ask yourself:

- *Can you handle the isolation?* Not all distance learning occurs in isolation, but a lot of it does. Are you the kind of people-oriented person who will miss the company of others? Perhaps, however, you can fulfill your needs for socializing through chat rooms and threaded discussions.

- *Are you a technology illiterate?* It's possible to be in a traditional class and not need to know anything about the Internet or the World Wide Web. But this is becoming less and less the case with distance learning. Do you need help in this department? All of Chapter 2 is devoted to this subject.
- *Can you give this the time required?* If you're holding a job, raising children, commuting long distances, or otherwise laboring under a lot of non-school kinds of demands, do you have the time to give to this course? Time management is such an important matter that we devote an entire chapter to it (Chapter 3).
- *Can you work on your own?* Clearly, with DL you're much more on your own than with traditional in-classroom courses. Do you think you have the discipline to perform the kinds of tasks and assignments required? A lot of this discipline comes in learning to manage your time (again, see Chapter 3).
- *Do you have good study skills?* We'd guess that you've already spent a considerable amount of your life in school. But are you good at it? Learning good study skills is important no matter how instructional material is delivered. But it's particularly important in distance learning, and that's why both Chapters 4 and 5 discuss the issue.

However you answered these questions, we hope you won't give up—at least right away. The rest of this book is designed to give you the kind of tools needed to become a distance learner. And to become a rip-roaring success at it.

INFORMATION TECHNOLOGY

The Mind Tools of Cyberspace

With traditional learning, you simply show up at a classroom and start taking notes or joining in discussion. This is still the case with those forms of distance learning in which students and instructors deal with each other by mail or in telecourses. With Internet-based forms of instruction, however, a whole new set of skills is required, such as learning how to deal with e-mail and the World Wide Web. If you think your skills here need some boosting, this chapter is for you.°

ACCESSING THE INTERNET

Because of its standard interfaces and low rates, "the Internet has been the great leveler for communications—the way the PC was for computing," says Boston analyst Virginia Brooks. To gain access to the Internet, you need three things: (1) an *access device,* such as a personal computer with a modem; (2) a *physical connection,* such as a telephone line; and (3) an *Internet service provider (ISP).*

Can you watch movies or television on any Internet-connected PC? Perhaps you can if you're fortunate enough to be in a state-of-the-art college dorm with 24/7 high-bandwidth Internet access. **_Bandwidth_ is an expression of how much data—text, voice, video, and so on—can be sent through a communications channel in a given amount of time.** A college dormitory wired with coaxial or fiber-optic cable will have more bandwidth than will a house out in the country served by conventional copper-wire telephone lines; access to information will be hundreds of times faster in the dorm. Most distance learning students are not privileged to have this kind of broadband or high-speed access.

Data are transmitted in characters, or collections of bits. Data-transmission speeds today are measured in the following terms:

°Chapter adapted from Brian K. Williams & Stacey C. Sawyer, *Using Information Technology: A Practical Introduction to Computers & Communications—Complete Version,* 5th ed. (Burr Ridge, IL: McGraw-Hill/Irwin, 2002), Chap. 2. By permission of McGraw-Hill.

- **_bps_ (bits per second):** A computer with an older modem might have a speed of 28,800 bps.
- **_Kbps_ (kilobits per second):** This, the most frequently used measure, means 1,000 bits per second. The speed of a modem that is 28,800 bps might be expressed as 28.8 Kbps.
- **_Mbps_ (megabits per second):** A megabit is 1 million bits.
- **_Gbps_ (gigabits per second):** A gigabit is 1 billion bits.

Why is it important to know these terms? Because the number of bits affects how fast you can upload to or download information from a remote computer. **_Downloading_ is transmitting data from a remote computer to a local computer,** as from your school or company's mainframe to your own PC. **_Uploading_ is transmitting data from a local computer to a remote computer.**

Assuming you have no access to a school or corporate network, what are your choices of **_physical connection_—the wired or wireless means of connecting to the Internet?** A lot depends on where you live. As you might expect, urban and many suburban areas offer more broadband connections than rural areas do. Among the principal means of connection are (1) telephone (dial-up) modem, (2) several kinds of high-speed phone lines—ISDN, DSL, or T1, (3) cable modem, and (4) wireless—satellite and other through-the-air links.

Let's consider the various kinds of services and the connections they offer.

Telephone (Dial-Up) Modem: Low Speed but Inexpensive & Widely Available

A telephone _modem_ is a device that sends and receives data over telephone lines to and from computers. This is known as a *dial-up* connection. These days, the modem is generally installed inside your computer, but there are also external modems. The modem is attached to the telephone wall outlet.

Most modems today have a maximum speed of 56 Kbps. That doesn't mean that you'll be sending and receiving data at that rate. The modem in your computer must negotiate with the modems used by your Internet service provider (ISP), the organization that actually connects you to the Internet, which may have modems operating at slower speeds, such as 28.8 Kbps. In addition, lower-quality phone lines or heavy traffic during peak hours—such as 5 P.M. to 11 P.M. in residential areas—can slow down your rate of transmission.

One disadvantage of a telephone modem is that while you're online you can't use your phone to make voice calls. In addition, people who try to call you while you're using the modem will get a busy signal. (Call waiting will also interrupt an online connection, so you need to check with your phone company about how to disable it.) As we discuss under "Internet Service Providers" (page 24), you probably won't need to pay long-distance phone rates, because most ISPs offer local access numbers. The cost of a dial-up modem connection to the ISP is $0–$30 per month, plus a possible setup charge of $10–$25.

High-Speed Phone Lines: More Expensive but Available in Most Cities

Waiting while your computer's modem takes 25 minutes to transmit a 1-minute low-quality video from a Website may have you pummeling the desk in frustration. To get some relief, you could enhance your POTS (for "plain old telephone system") connection with a high-speed adaptation or get a new, dedicated line. Among the choices are ISDN, DSL, and T1, available in most major cities, though not in rural and many suburban areas.

ISDN LINE   _ISDN_—**for _integrated services digital network_—consists of hardware and software that allows voice, video, and data to be communicated over traditional copper-wire telephone lines.** Capable of transmitting up to 128 Kbps, ISDN is able to send signals over POTS lines. If you were trying to download an approximately 6-minute-long music video from the World Wide Web, it would take you about 4 hours and 45 minutes with a 28.8-Kbps modem. An ISDN connection would reduce this to an hour.

ISDN costs $40–$110 a month to the phone company and the Internet service provider. In addition, you may need to pay your phone company $350–$700 or so to hook up an ISDN connector box, possibly run in a new phone line, and install the necessary software in your PC.

DSL LINE   _DSL_—**for _digital subscriber line_—also uses regular phone lines, but can transmit data in megabits per second.** Incoming data flow is significantly faster than outgoing data. That is, your computer can _receive_ data at the rate of 1.5–8.4 Mbps, but it can _send_ data at only 16–640 Kbps. This arrangement may be fine, however, if you're principally interested in obtaining very large amounts of data (video, music) rather than in sending them to others. With DSL, you can download that 6-minute music video in only 11 minutes (compared to an hour with ISDN). A big advantage of DSL is that it is always on and, unlike cable (discussed below), its transmission rate is consistent. One-time installation cost is $100–$200 plus $100–$300 for a modem supplied by the phone company, and the monthly cost is $40–$300.

There is one big drawback to DSL: You have to live within 3.3 miles of a phone company central switching office, because the access speed and reliability degrade with distance. However, phone companies are building thousands of remote switching facilities to enhance service throughout their regions. Another drawback is that you have to choose from a list of Internet service providers that are under contract to the phone company you use, although other DSL providers exist.

T1 LINE   If you're taking a distance learning course at work, you might have access to a **_T1 line_, essentially a traditional trunk line that carries 24 normal telephone circuits and has a transmission rate of 1.5 Kbps.** Generally, T1 lines are used by corporate, government, and academic sites.

Cable Modem: Close Competitor to DSL

If DSL's 11 minutes to move a 6-minute video sounds good, 2 minutes sounds even better. That's the rate of transmission for cable modems, which can transmit outgoing data at 500 Kbps and incoming data at 10 Mbps (and eventually, it's predicted, at 30 Mbps). **A _cable modem_ connects a personal computer to a cable-TV system that offers an Internet connection.** With around 1 million subscribers, cable has been rapidly gaining market share in high-speed delivery services. Like a DSL connection, it is always on; unlike DSL, you don't need to live near a switching station. Costing $30–$60 a month plus installation and equipment ($300–$500), cable is available in most major cities.

A disadvantage, however, is that because you and your neighbors are sharing the system, during peak-load times your service may be slowed to the speed of a regular dial-up modem. (You're also more vulnerable to attacks from hackers, although there are defensive or "firewall" programs, such as Winproxy, that reduce the risk.) Finally, cable companies may force you to use their own Internet service providers.

Wireless Systems: Satellite & Other Through-the-Air Connections

Suppose you live out in the country and you're tired of the molasses-like speed of your cranky local phone system. You might consider taking to the air.

SATELLITE   With a pizza-size satellite dish on your roof, you can receive data at the rate of 400 Kbps from a **_communications satellite_, a space station that transmits radio waves (called "microwaves") from Earth-based stations.** Unfortunately, your outgoing transmission will still be only 56 Kbps, because you'll have to use your phone line for that purpose, although genuine two-way satellite service is under development (as from DirectPC). Equipment available from InfoDish or PC Connection costs about $190; installation runs $100–$250; and monthly charges (including ISP charges) are $30–$130, depending on how much time you spend online.

OTHER WIRELESS CONNECTIONS   In urban areas, some businesses are using radio waves transmitted between towers that handle cellular phone calls, which can send data at up to 155 Mbps and are not only fast and dependable but also always on. The cost is $159–$1,400 a month, depending on speed. However, because your antenna must be within line of sight of the service's base station, this system is not available outside cities. Perhaps more practical and affordable is wireless technology such as that to be offered by AT&T (though only in areas not served by its TCI cable service), which enables you to send and receive data (at 512 Kbps) from a box on the outside wall of your house; it does not require line-of-sight—that is, unimpeded—connection with the base station.

INTERNET SERVICE PROVIDERS

Suppose you have an access device (such as a modem) and you've signed up for a wired or wireless connection. Next, unless you're already on a school or corporate network, you'll need to arrange for an ***Internet service provider,* or *ISP,* a company that connects you through your communications line to its server, or central computer, which connects you to the Internet.** Some well-known ISPs are America Online (AOL, which is also a portal or proprietary network, as we explain below), EarthLink, Microsoft Network (MSN), AT&T WorldNet, and Prodigy. There are also many local ISPs. (To do some comparison shopping, go online to *www.thelist.com,* which lists ISPs from all over the world and will guide you through the process of finding one that's best for you. Also, see the box on the following page.) If you don't have an ISP, you can access the Internet through a library or corporate terminal.

Once you have contacted an ISP and paid the required fee (it's usually charged to your credit card), the ISP will provide you with information about phone numbers for a local connection. This connection is called *"a point of presence (POP)."* The ISP will also provide you with communications software for setting up your computer and modem to connect with them. For this you use your *user name* (also called "user ID") and your *password,* a secret word or string of characters that enables you to **_log on,_ or make a connection to the remote computer.** You will also need to get yourself an e-mail address, as we discuss next.

USING E-MAIL

Once connected with an ISP, most people want to immediately join the millions of users who send and receive electronic mail. E-mail is stored in your mailbox on the ISP's **_server,_ a central computer that holds collections of data and programs for connecting PCs and other devices linked to the network.** When you use your e-mail software to retrieve your messages, the e-mail is sent from the server to your computer. E-mail can be sent at any time and to several people simultaneously. You can receive e-mail wherever you are, using your user name and password to connect to the Internet. In addition, you can attach long (or short) documents or other materials to your e-mail message.

E-MAIL SOFTWARE AND CARRIERS   If you aren't on a school or corporate network, there are four ways to go about getting and sending e-mail:

- *Buy e-mail software.* Popular e-mail software programs are Eudora, Outlook Express, or Lotus Notes. However, you may not need to spend money on these programs because of the following alternatives.
- *Get an e-mail program as part of other computer software.* When you buy a new computer, the system will probably include e-mail software, perhaps as part of the software (called *browsers*) used to search the World

Choosing an Internet Service Provider

If you belong to a college or company, you may get an ISP free. (We assume you have your employer's permission to use a company computer for DL purposes.) Some public libraries also offer freenet connections.

Here are some important questions to ask when you're making those phone calls to locate an Internet service provider:[1]

Costs
- Is there a setup fee? (Most ISPs no longer charge this, though some "free" ISPs will.)
- How much is unlimited access per month? (Most charge about $20 for unlimited usage, but inquire about free or low-cost trial memberships or discounts for long-term commitments.)
- If access is supposedly free, what are the trade-offs besides putting up with heavy advertising? (For instance, if the ISP closely monitors your activity in order to accurately target ads, what guarantees do you have that information about you will be kept private? What charges will you face if you try to scrap the advertising window or drop the service?)
- Is there a contract, and for what length of time? That is, are you obligated to stick with the ISP for a while even if you're unhappy with it?

Access
- Is the access number a local phone call? (If not, your monthly long-distance phone tolls could exceed the ISP fee.)
- Is there an alternative dial-up number if the main number is out of service?
- Is access available when you're traveling? Your provider should offer either a wide range of local access numbers in the cities you tend to visit or toll-free numbers.

Support
- What kind of help does the ISP give in setting up your connection?
- Is there free, 24-hour technical support? Is it reachable through via a toll-free telephone call?
- How difficult is it to reach tech support? (Try calling the number before you sign up for the ISP and see how long it takes to get a response. Many ISPs keep customers on hold for a long time.)

Reliability
- What is the average connection success rate for users trying to connect on the first try? (The industry average call-success rate is 93.1%. You can try dialing the number during peak hours, to see if you get a modem screech, which is good, rather than a busy signal, which is bad. You can also check Visual Networks, www.inversenet.com, for call-failure/call-success rates of various ISPs.)
- Will the ISP keep up with technology? (Is it planning to offer broadband technology, such as DSL, for speedier access?)
- Will the ISP sell your name to marketers or bombard you with junk messages (spam)?

Wide Web, such as Internet Explorer or Netscape Communicator. An example is Microsoft's Outlook Express, which is part of its Explorer software bundle.

- **Get e-mail software as part of your ISP package.** Internet service providers—AOL, Prodigy, EarthLink, AT&T WorldNet—provide e-mail software for their subscribers.
- **Get free e-mail services.** These are available from a variety of sources, ranging from so-called portals or Internet gateways (such as Yahoo!, Excite, or Lycos) to cable-TV channel CNN's Website.

E-MAIL ADDRESSES   You'll need an e-mail address, of course, a sort of electronic mailbox used to send and receive messages. All such addresses follow the same format: *user@domain.* A ***domain*** **is simply an electronic location on the Internet.** Consider the following address:

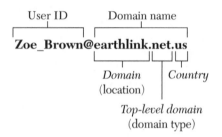

Let's look at the elements of this address.

   Zoe_Brown   The first section, the *user ID*, identifies who is at the address—in this case, *Zoe_Brown.* (Zoe Brown's user name might be variously designated with and without capital letters, as follows: *Zoe_Brown, zoe_brown, zoe.brown, zoebrown, zbrown, zoeb,* and so on.)

   The second section, the *domain name*, which appears after the @ (called "at") symbol, tells the location and type of address. Domain-name components are separated by periods (called "dots") and identify the target server, as follows:

   @earthlink   The *domain* portion of the address (such as EarthLink, an Internet service provider) provides specific information about the server to which the message should be delivered. This is simply a computer, which could be physically located anywhere.

   .net   The *top-level domain* is a three-letter extension that describes the *domain type:* the extensions *.net, .com, .gov, .edu, .org, .mil,* and *.int* mean network, commercial, government, educational, nonprofit, military, or international organization, respectively.

   .us   Some domain names also include a two-letter extension for the country in which the server is located—for example, *.us* for United States, *.ca* for Canada, *.uk* for United Kingdom, *.jp* for Japan, *.tr* for Turkey.

   Sometimes you'll see an address in which people have their own domains—for example, *Zoe@Brown.com.* However, you can't simply make up a domain name; it has to be registered. (You can check on whether an address is available and register it by checking *www.register.com* or *www.internicregistrations.com*)

Incidentally, many people who are unhappy with their ISPs don't change, because they don't want to have to notify their friends of a new e-mail address. However, you can switch ISPs by using an e-mail forwarding service (such as Pobox.com, or a college alumni group that offers lifetime e-mail addresses). That way, you can keep one e-mail address no matter how many times you change providers.

Some tips about using e-mail addresses:

- ***Type addresses carefully.*** You need to type the address *exactly* as it appears, including all spaces, underscores, and periods. If you type an e-mail address incorrectly, your message will be returned to you with a header of (to most people) incomprehensible strings of characters.
- ***Use the Reply command.*** When responding to an e-message someone has sent you, the easiest way to avoid making address mistakes is to use the *Reply* command, which will automatically fill in the correct address in the "To" line. (Avoid the *Reply to All* command unless you want your answer to reach everyone who received the original message.)
- ***Use the "address book" feature.*** You can store the e-mail addresses of people sending you messages in your program's address book. This feature also allows you to organize your e-mail addresses according to a nickname or the person's real name so that, for instance, you can look up your friend Zoe Brown under her real name, instead of under her user name, *bugsme2,* which you might not remember. The address book also allows you to organize addresses into various groups—such as your friends, your parents, club members—so you can easily send all members of a group the same message with a single command.
- ***Deal with e-mail only once.*** When a message comes in, delete it, respond to it, or file it away in a folder. Don't use your inbox for storage.

ATTACHMENTS　You have written a great research paper and you immediately want to show it off to someone. If you were sending it via the U.S. Postal Service, you would write a cover note—"Hey, everyone: look at this great paper I wrote about term-paper cheating! See attached."—then attach it to the paper, and stick it in an envelope. E-mail has its own version of this. If the file of your paper exists in the computer from which you are sending e-mail, you can write your e-mail message (your cover note) and then use the *Attach File* command to attach the document.

Note: It's important that the person receiving the e-mail attachment have the same software that created the attached file, such as Microsoft Word, or have software that can read and convert the file.

Although you could also copy your document into the main message and send it that way, e-mail tends to lose formatting options such as **bold** or *italic* text or special symbols. And if you're sending song lyrics or poetry, the lines of text may break differently on someone else's display screen from how they do on yours. Thus, the benefit of the attachment feature is that it preserves all such formatting, provided the recipient is using the same word processing software that you did to write your paper. (If your e-mail is written in hypertext markup language, or HTML, the code designed for making Web pages, as we shall discuss, you can add special fonts, images, and colors to your messages.)

You can also attach pictures, sounds, videos, and other files to your e-mail message.

Note: Many *viruses*—those rogue programs that can seriously damage your PC or programs—ride along with e-mail as attached files. Thus, you should never open an attached file from an unknown source.

INSTANT MESSAGING   Instant messages are like a cross between e-mail and phone, allowing for communication that is far speedier than conventional e-mail. With ***instant messaging (IM),* any user on a given e-mail system can send a message and have it pop up instantly on the screen of anyone else logged onto that system.** Then, if both parties agree, they can initiate online typed conversations in real time. The messages appear on the display screen in a small ***window***—**a rectangular area containing a document or activity**—so that users can exchange messages almost instantaneously while operating other programs. Eventually, there will probably be an "open standard" so that anyone can send instant messages to anyone else, no matter what system people are on.

Examples of present instant-message systems are AOL Instant Messenger, also called "AIM" (AOL pioneered the idea by allowing members to add other members' names to a "Buddy List"), ICQ (for "I seek you," also from AOL), MSN Messenger, Prodigy Instant Messaging, Tribal Voice PowWow, and Yahoo Messenger. Some systems, such as Yahoo!'s, allow voice chats among users, if their PCs are equipped with microphones and speakers.

To get instant messaging, which is available for free, you download software and register with the service, providing it with a user name and password. You can then create a list of buddies with whom you want to communicate regularly. When your computer is connected to the Internet, the software checks in with a central server, which verifies your identity and looks to see if any of your buddies are also online. You can then start a conversation by sending a message to any buddy currently online.

MAILING LISTS: E-MAIL–BASED DISCUSSION GROUPS   Want to receive e-mail from people all over the world who share your interests? You can try finding a mailing list and then subscribing—signing up, just as you would for a free newsletter or magazine. ***Listservs* are e-mail mailing lists of people who regularly participate in discussion topics.** To subscribe, you send an e-mail to the listserv moderator and ask to become a member, after which you will automatically receive e-mail messages from anyone who responds to the server. A directory of mailing lists is available at Publicly Accessible Mailing Lists (*http://paml.net*) or Yahoo!'s OneList (*www.onelist.com*).

NETIQUETTE: APPROPRIATE ONLINE BEHAVIOR   New Internet users, known as *newbies,* may accidentally offend other people in a discussion group or in an e-mail simply because they are unaware of ***netiquette,* or "network etiquette"—appropriate online behavior.** In general, netiquette has two basic rules: (1) don't waste people's time, and (2) don't say anything to a person online that you wouldn't say to his or her face.

Some more specific rules of netiquette are as follows:

- **Consult FAQs.** Most online groups post **_FAQs_—for _frequently asked questions_—that explain expected norms of online behavior for a particular group.** Always read these first—before someone in the group tells you you've made a mistake.
- **Avoid flaming.** A form of speech unique to online communication, **_flaming_ is writing an online message that uses derogatory, obscene, or inappropriate language.** Flaming is a form of public humiliation inflicted on people who have failed to read FAQs or otherwise not observed netiquette (although it can happen just because the sender has poor impulse control and needs a course in anger management). Something that smooths communication online is the use of **_emoticons_, keyboard-produced pictorial representations of expressions.** Examples are :-) (happy face), :-((sorrow or frown), <g> (grin), and LOL (laugh out loud). Other common abbreviations include BTW (by the way), IMHO (in my humble opinion), and FYI (for your information).
- **Don't SHOUT.** Use of all-capital letters is considered the equivalent of SHOUTING. Avoid, except when they are required for emphasis (as when you can't use italics or boldface in your e-messages).
- **Avoid sloppiness, but avoid criticizing others' sloppiness.** Avoid spelling and grammatical errors. But don't criticize those same errors in others' messages. (After all, they may not be English native speakers.) Most e-mail software comes with spell-checking capability, which is easy to use.
- **Don't send huge file attachments, unless requested.** Your fellow online student living in the country may find it takes minutes rather than seconds for his or her computer to download a massive file (as of a book-length paper you want to share). This may tie up the system at a time when that person badly needs to use it. Better to query in advance before sending large files as attachments. Also, whenever you send an attachment, be sure the recipient has the appropriate software to open your attachment (you both are using Microsoft Word, for example).
- **When replying, quote only the relevant portion.** If you're replying to just a couple of matters in a long e-mail posting, don't send back the entire message (which may happen if you simply use the _Reply_ command). This forces your recipient to wade through lots of text to find the reference. Instead, edit his or her original text down to the relevant paragraph and then put in your response immediately following.

USING FILTERS TO SORT YOUR E-MAIL   One way to stay on top of the steady stream of e-mail is to use _filters,_ which are instant organizers, using the name of the person or the mailing list to put that particular mail into one folder. Then you can read e-mails sent to this folder later when you have time, freeing up your inbox for mail that needs your more immediate attention. Instructions on how to set up filters are in your e-mail program's Help section.

SPAM: UNWANTED JUNK E-MAIL   *Spam* **refers to unsolicited e-mail in the form of advertising or chain letters.** Usually you won't recognize the sender on your list of incoming mail, and often the subject line will give no hint, stating something such as "The status of your application" or "It's up to you now." The solicitations can range from money-making schemes to online pornography.

Some ways to deal with this nuisance are as follows:

- ***Delete without opening the message.*** Opening the spam message can actually send a signal to the spammer that someone has looked at the onscreen message and therefore that the e-mail address is valid—which means you'll probably get more spams in the future. If you don't recognize the name on your inbox directory or the topic on the inbox subject line, you can simply delete the message without reading it. Or you can use a preview feature in your e-mail program to look at the message without actually opening it, then delete it. (*Hint:* Be sure to get rid of all the deleted messages from time to time, which otherwise will build up in your "trash" area.)
- ***Never reply to a spam message!*** The following advice needs to be taken seriously: *Never reply in any way to a spam message!* Replying confirms to the spammer that yours is an active e-mail address. Some spam senders will tell you that if you want to be removed from their mailing list, you should type the word REMOVE or UNSUBSCRIBE in the subject line and use the *Reply* command to send it back. Invariably, however, all this does is confirm to the spammer that your address is valid, setting you up to receive more unsolicited messages.
- ***Enlist the help of your ISP or use spam filters.*** Your ISP may offer a spam filter to stop the stuff before you even see it. If it doesn't, you can sign up for a filtering service, such as ImagiNet (*www.imagin.net*) for a small monthly charge. Or there are do-it-yourself spam-stopping programs. *Examples:* Brightmail (*www.brightmail.com*), Novasoft SpamKiller (*www.spamkiller. com*), High Mountain Software SpamEater Pro (*www.hms.com*). Be warned, however: Even so-called spam killers don't always work.
- ***Fight back.*** If you want to try to get back at spammers, check with abuse.net (*www.abuse.net*) or Ed Falk's Spam Tracking Page (*www.rahul.net/falk*). These will tell you where to report spammers, the appropriate people to complain to, and other spam-fighting tips.

WHAT ABOUT KEEPING E-MAIL PRIVATE?   The single best piece of advice that can be given about sending e-mail is this: *Pretend every electronic message is a postcard that can be read by anyone*—because the chances are high that it could be. (This includes e-mail on school or campus systems as well.)

THE WORLD WIDE WEB

"I found my old elementary-school buddy by surfing the Internet."

When people talk about the Internet in this way, they really mean exploring the World Wide Web. After e-mail, visiting sites ("surfing") on the Web is the most

popular use of the Internet. What makes the World Wide Web so graphically invit-
ing and easily navigable is that this international collection of servers (1) contains
information in multimedia form and (2) is connected by hypertext links.

- *Multimedia form:* Whereas e-mail messages are generally text, the Web
  provides information in **_multimedia_ form—graphics, video, and audio as
  well as text.** You can see color pictures, animation, and full-motion video.
  You can download music. You can listen to radio broadcasts. You can have
  telephone conversations with others.
- *Use of hypertext:* Whereas with e-mail you can connect only with specific
  addresses you know about, with the Web you have **_hypertext_, which is a
  system that links documents scattered across many Internet sites.** It
  makes a word or phrase in one document into a connection to a document in
  a different place. The format, or language, used on the Web is **_hypertext
  markup language_, abbreviated HTML. It is the set of special instructions (called "tags" or "markups") that are used to specify document
  structure,** formatting, and links to other documents.
- *Web surfing for beginners:* For example, if you were reading this book
  onscreen, you could use your mouse to click on the word "multimedia"—
  which would be highlighted—in the paragraph above, and that would lead
  you to another location, where perhaps "multimedia" is defined—with text,
  pictures, sound, or all three. Then you could click on a word in that definition, and that would lead you to more related material.

  The result is that one term or phrase will lead to another, and so you can
  access all kinds of databases and libraries all over the world. Among the
  droplets in what amounts to a Niagara Falls of information available:
  Weather maps and forecasts. Guitar chords. Recipe archives. Sports schedules. Daily newspapers in all kinds of languages. Nielsen television ratings. A
  ZIP code guide. Works of literature. The Alcoholism Research Data Base.
  U.S. government phone numbers. The Central Intelligence Agency world
  map. The daily White House press releases. And on and on.

The Web & How It Works

If a Rip Van Winkle fell asleep in 1989 (the year computer scientist Tim Berners-
Lee developed the Web software) and awoke today, he would be completely
baffled by the new vocabulary that we now encounter on an almost daily basis:
Website, home page, www. Let's see how we would explain to him what these and
similar Web terms mean:

- *Website—the domain on the computer:* You'll recall we described top-
  level domains (such as *.com, .edu, .org,* and *.net*) in our discussion of e-mail
  addresses. **A computer with a domain name is called a _site_.** When you
  decide to buy books at the online site of bookseller Barnes & Noble, you
  would visit its Website at *www.barnesandnoble.com;* the Website is the
  location of a Web domain name in a computer somewhere on the Internet.
  More usefully, a **_Website_ is a collection of electronic documents.**

- **Web pages—the documents on a Website:** A Website is composed of a Web page or collection of related Web pages. A **Web page is a document on the World Wide Web that can include text, pictures, sound, and video.** The first page you see at a Website is like the title page of a book. This is the **home page, or welcome page, which identifies the Website and contains links to other pages at the site.** If you have your own personal Website, it might consist of just one page—the home page. Large Websites have scores or even hundreds of pages. (The contents of home pages often change. Or they may disappear, so that the connecting links to them in other Web pages become links to nowhere.)
- **Browsers—software for connecting with Websites:** A **Web browser (or simply browser) is software that enables users to view Web pages and to jump from one page to another.** The two most well-known browsers are Microsoft's Internet Explorer, which most users prefer, and Netscape Communicator, once the leader but now used by only about a third of consumers. When you connect to a particular Website with your browser, the first thing you will see is the home page. Then, using your mouse, you can move from one page to another by clicking on hypertext links.
- **URLs—addresses for Web pages:** Before your browser can connect with a Website, it needs to know the site's address, the URL. **The URL—for Uniform Resource Locator—is a string of characters that points to a specific piece of information anywhere on the Web.** A URL consists of (1) the Web *protocol*, (2) the name of the Web *server*, (3) the *directory* (or folder) on that server, and (4) the *file* within that directory (perhaps with an *extension,* such as *html* or *htm*). Usually you need to type a URL *exactly* the way it appears—not type a capital letter, for instance, if a lowercase letter is indicated.

   Consider the following example of a URL for a Website offered by the National Park Service for Yosemite National Park:

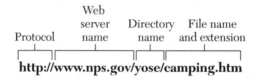

                                 Web
                                 server   Directory File name
             Protocol   name   name and extension

http://www.nps.gov/yose/camping.htm

Let's look at each element.

   http:// A ***protocol* is a set of communication rules for exchanging information.** When you see the *http://* at the beginning of some Web addresses (as in *http://www.wadsworth.com*), that stands for ***HTTP,* for *hypertext transfer protocol*, the communications rules that allow browsers to connect with Web servers.**

   Note: Most browsers assume that all Web addresses begin with *http://* and so you don't need to type this part; just start with whatever follows, such as *www.*

   www.nps.gov/ The *Web server* is the particular computer on which this Website is located. The *www* stands for "World Wide Web," of course; the

.nps stands for "National Park Service," and the *.gov* is the top-level domain name indicating that this is a government Website. The server might be physically located in Yosemite National Park in California; in the Park Service's headquarters in Washington, D.C.; or somewhere else entirely.

yose/   The *directory* name is the name on the server for the directory, or folder, from which you need to pull the file. Here it is *yose* for "Yosemite." For Yellowstone National Park, it is *yell.*

camping.htm   The *file* is the particular page or document that you are seeking. Here it is *camping.htm,* because you have gone to a Web page about Yosemite's camping facilities. The .htm is an extension to the file name, and this extension informs the browser that the file is an HTML file.

A URL, you may have observed, is *not* the same thing as an e-mail address. Some people might type in *president@whitehouse.gov.us* and expect to get a Website, but it won't happen. The Website for the White House (which includes presidential information, history, a tour, and guide to federal services) is *http:// www.whitehouse.gov*

Using Your Browser to Get Around the Web

The World Wide Web now consists of an estimated 1 billion Web pages. Moreover, the Web is constantly changing; more sites are created and old ones are retired. Without a browser and various kinds of search tools, we could not begin to make any kind of sense of this enormous amount of data.

As mentioned, a Web page may include *hyperlinks*—words and phrases that appear as underlined or color text—that are connections to other Web pages. You click on the hyperlink text, and the linked page appears onscreen. On a home page, for instance, the hyperlinks serve to connect the top page with other pages throughout the Website. Other hyperlinks will connect to other pages on other Websites, whether located on a computer next door or one on the other side of the world.

If you buy a new computer, it will come with a browser already installed. Most browsers have a similar look and feel. Here we discuss Microsoft Internet Explorer, which appears on many computers.

The Explorer browser screen has five basic elements: *menu bar, toolbar, URL bar, workspace,* and *status bar.* To execute menu bar and toolbar commands, you use the mouse to move the pointer over the word, known as a *menu selection,* and click the left button of the mouse. This will result in a *pull-down menu* of other commands for other options.

After you've been using a mouse for a while, you may find moving the pointer around somewhat time-consuming. As a shortcut, if you click on the right mouse button, you can reach many of the commands on the toolbar (*Back, Forward,* and so on) via a pop-up menu.

- **Starting out from home:** The first page you see when you start up your browser is the *home page* or *start page.* You can choose any page on the Web you want as your start page, but a good start page offers links to sites you want to visit frequently. Often you may find that the ISP with which you arrange your Internet connection will provide its own start page. However, you'll no doubt be able to customize it to make it your own personal home page.

- **Personalizing your home page:** Want to see the weather forecast for your hometown area when you first log on? Or your horoscope, "message of the day," or the day's news (general, sports, financial, health, or lottery results)? Or the Websites you visit most frequently? Or a reminder page (that lists deadlines or people's birthdays)? You can probably personalize your home page following the directions provided with the first start page you encounter. Or if you have an older Microsoft or Netscape browser, you can get a customizing system from either company. A customized start page is also provided by Yahoo!, Excite, AltaVista, and similar services.
- **Getting around—Back, Forward, Home, and Search features:** Driving in a foreign city (or even Boston or San Francisco) can be an interesting experience in which street names change, turns lead into unknown neighborhoods, and signs aren't always evident, so that soon you have no idea where you are. That's what the Internet is like, although on a far more massive scale. Fortunately, unlike being lost in Rome, surfing the Net provides navigational aids on your browser toolbar: The *Back* command icon takes you back to the previous page. *Forward* lets you look again at a page you returned from. If you really get lost, you can start over by clicking on *Home,* which returns you to your home page. *Search* lists various other search tools, as we will describe. Other navigational aides are history lists and bookmarks.
- **History lists:** If you are browsing through many Web pages, it can be difficult to keep track of the locations of the pages you've already visited. The *history list* allows you to quickly return to the pages you have recently visited.
- **Bookmarks or favorites:** One great helper for finding your way is the *bookmark* or *favorites* system, which lets you store the URLs of Web pages you frequently visit so that you don't have to remember and retype their addresses. Say you're visiting a site that you really like and that you know you'd like to come back to. You click on your *Bookmark* or *Favorites* feature, which displays the URL on your screen, then click on *Add,* which automatically stores the address. Later you can locate the site name on your bookmark menu, click on it, and the site will reappear. (When you want to delete it, you can use the right mouse button and select the *Delete* command.)
- **Interactivity—hyperlinks, radio buttons, and fill-in text boxes:** There are three possible ways to interact with a Web page—sometimes all three are used on the same page:
  (1) By using your mouse to click on the hyperlinks, which will transfer you to another Web page.
  (2) By using your mouse to click on a *radio button* and then clicking on a *Submit* command or pressing the Enter key. **<ins>Radio buttons</ins> are little circles located in front of various options; selecting an option with the mouse places a dot in the corresponding circle.**

(3) By typing text into a fill-in text box, then pressing the Enter key or clicking on a *Go* or *Continue* command, which will transfer you to another Web page.

- ***Scrolling and frames:*** To the bottom and side of your screen display, you will note __*scroll arrows*__, **small up/down and left/right arrows. Clicking on scroll arrows with your mouse pointer moves the screen so that you can see the rest of the Web page, a movement known as __scrolling__.** You can also use the arrow keys on your keyboard for scrolling.

  Some Web pages are divided into different rectangles known as frames, each with its own scroll arrows. **A __*frame*__ is an independently controllable section of a Web page.** A Web page might be divided into separate frames, each with different features or options.

- ***Looking at two pages simultaneously:*** If you want to look at more than one Web page at the same time, you can position them side by side on your display screen. Select *New* from your File menu to open more than one browser window.

WEB PORTALS: STARTING POINTS FOR FINDING INFORMATION

Using a browser is like exploring an enormous cave with flashlight and string. You point your flashlight at something, go there, and at that location you can see another place to go to; meanwhile, you're unrolling the ball of string behind you, so that you can find your way back.

But what if you want to visit only the most spectacular rock formations in the cave and skip the rest? For that you need a guidebook. There are many such "guidebooks" for finding information on the Web: Internet superstations known as __**Web portals**__, **which are Websites that group together popular features such as search tools, e-mail, electronic commerce, and discussion groups.** The most popular portals are America Online, Yahoo!, Microsoft Network, Infoseek, Snap, Netscape, Lycos, Go Network, Excite Network, AltaVista, and WebCrawler.

Starting Your Search

When you log on to a portal, you can do three things: (1) check the home page for general information, (2) use the directories to find a topic you want, or (3) use a keyword to search for a topic.

- ***Check the home page for general information.*** You can treat a portal's home or start page as you would one of the mass media—something you tune in to in order to get news headlines, weather forecasts, sports scores, stock-price indexes, and today's horoscope. You might also proceed past the home page to check your e-mail, if you happen to be using the portal for this purpose.

- ***Use the directories to find a topic.*** Before they acquired their other features, many of these portals began as a type of search tool known as a *directory*, **providing lists of several categories of Websites classified by topic,** such as *Business & Finance* or *Health & Fitness.* Such a category is also called a "hypertext index," and its purpose is to allow you to access information in specific categories by clicking on a hypertext link.

The initial general categories in Yahoo!, for instance, are *Arts & Humanities, Business & Economy, Computers & Internet, Education, Government, Health,* and so on. Using your mouse to click on one general category (such as *Recreation & Sports*) will lead you to another category (such as *Sports*), which in turn will lead you to another category (such as *College & University*), and on to another category (such as *Conferences*), and so on, down through the hierarchy. If you do this long enough, you will "drill down" through enough categories that you will find the document (Website) on the topic you want.

Unfortunately, not everything can be so easily classified in hierarchical form. A faster way may be to do a *keyword search.*

- **Use keyword to search for a topic.** At the top of each portal's home page is a blank space into which you can type a ***keyword*, the subject word or words of the topic you wish to find.** If you want a biography on former San Francisco football quarterback Joe Montana, then *Joe Montana* is the keyword. This way you don't have to plow through menu after menu of subject categories. The results of your keyword search will be displayed in a short summary of documents containing the keyword you typed.

Many users are increasingly bypassing the better-known Web portals and going directly to specialty sites or small portals, such as those featuring education, finance, and sports. Examples are Webstart Communications' computer and communications site (*www.cmpcmm.com/cc*), Travel.com's travel site (*www.travel.com/sitemap.htm*), and the *New York Times* home page used by the paper's own newsroom staff to find journalism-related sites (*www.nytimes.com/library/tech/reference/cynavi.html*). Some colleges are also installing portals for their students.

Four Types of Search Engines

When you use a keyword to search for a topic, you are using a piece of software known as a search engine. Whereas directories are lists of Websites classified by topic (as offered by portals), ***search engines* allow you to find specific documents through keyword searches and menu choices.** The type of search engine you use depends on what you're looking for.

There are four types of such search tools: (1) human-organized, (2) computer-created, (3) hybrid, and (4) metasearch.[2]

- ***Human-organized search sites:*** If you're looking for a biography of Apple Computer founder Steve Jobs, a search engine based on human judgment is probably your best bet. Why? Because, unlike a computer-created search site, the search tool won't throw everything remotely associated with his name at you. More and more, the top five search sites on the Web (Yahoo!, AOL, MSN, Netscape, and Lycos) are going in the direction of human indexing. Unlike indexes created by computers, humans can judge data for relevance and categorize them in ways that are useful to you. Many of these sites hire people who are subject-area experts (with the idea that, for example, someone interested in gardening would be best able to organize gardening sites). Examples of human-organized search sites are Yahoo!, Open Directory, About.com, and LookSmart.

- **Computer-created search sites:** If you want to see what things show up next to Steve Jobs's name or every instance in which it appears, a computer-created search site may be best. These are assembled by software "spiders" that crawl all over the Web and send back reports to be collected and organized with little human intervention. The downside is that computer-created indexes may deliver you more information than you want. Examples of this type are Northern Light, Excite, WebCrawler, FAST Search, and Inktomi.

- **Hybrid search sites:** Hybrid sites generally use humans supplemented by computer indexes. The idea is to see that nothing falls through the cracks. All the principal sites are now hybrid: AOL Search, AltaVista, Lycos, MSN Search, and Netscape Search. Others are Ask Jeeves, Direct Hit, Go, GoTo.com, Google, HotBot, and Snap. Ask Jeeves pioneered the use of natural-language queries (you ask a question as you would to a person: "Where can I find a biography of Steve Jobs?"). Google ranks listings by popularity as well as by how well they match the request. GoTo ranks by who paid the most money for top billing.

- **Metasearch sites:** Metasearch sites send your query to several other different search tools and compile the results so as to present the broadest view. Examples are Go2Net/MetaCrawler, SavvySearch, Dogpile, Inference Find, ProFusion, Mamma, The Big Hub, and C4 TotalSearch.

The addresses for the principal Web portals are given in the box on page 38. (Your browser will automatically fill in *http://* before the *www*.)

Tips for Smart Searching

The phrase "trying to find a needle in a haystack" will come vividly to mind the first time you type a word into a search engine and back comes a response on the order of "63,173 listings found." Clearly, you need a strategy for narrowing your search. Following are some tips:

- **Start with general search tools.** Begin with general search tools such as those offered by AltaVista, Excite, GoTo.com, HotBot, Lycos, and Yahoo! (Later, if you haven't been able to narrow your search, you can go to specific search tools, as we'll describe.)

- **Choose your search terms well and watch your spelling.** Use the most precise words possible. If you're looking for information about novelist Thomas Wolfe (author of *Look Homeward Angel,* published 1929) rather than novelist/journalist Tom Wolfe (*A Man in Full,* 1998), details are important: Type *Thomas,* not *Tom; Wolfe,* not *Wolf.* Use *poodle* rather than *dog,*

Addresses for Principal Web Portals

About.com	www.about.com
AltaVista	www.altavista.com
AOL Search	search.aol.com
AskJeeves	www.ask.com
The Big Hub	www.thebighub.com
Britannica	www.britannica.com
C4 TotalSearch Technology	www.c4.com
Direct Hit	www.directhit.com
Dogpile	www.dogpile.com
Excite Network	www.excite.com
FAST Search	www.alltheweb.com
Go	www.go.com
Google	www.google.com
Google Groups	http://groups.google.com
GoTo	www.goto.com
Go2Net/Metacrawler	www.go2net.com
HotBot	www.hotbot.com
Inference Find	www.infind.com
Internet Public Library	www.ipl.org/col
Inktomi	www.inktomi.com
Ixquick Metasearch	www.ixquick.com
LookSmart	www.looksmart.com
Lycos	www.lycos.com
MSN Search	http://search.msn.com
Netscape Search	http://search.netscape.com
Northern Light	www.northernlight.com
Open Directory	http://dmoz.org
ProFusion	www.profusion.com
Scout Report Archives	http://scout.cs.wisc.edu/archives
Snap	www.snap.com
WebCrawler	www.webcrawler.com
Yahoo!	www.yahoo.com

The Internet Public Library gives the following advice about Web searching:

- If you're a new searcher, start with Yahoo!, Ask Jeeves, Google, Northern Light.
- If you're an experienced searcher, you could try Google, AltaVista, HotBot, Ixquick.
- If you prefer quality over quantity, use Google, Internet Public Library, Britannica, Scout Report Archives, About.com
- If you're looking for specific and arcane information, use Northern Light, Ixquick, Google Groups.

Maui rather than *Hawaii,* and *Martin guitar* rather than *guitar,* or you'll get thousands of responses that have little or nothing to do with what you're looking for. You may need to use several similar words to explore the topic you're investigating: *car racing, auto racing, NASCAR racing, drag racing, drag-racing, dragracing,* and so on.

- ***Use phrases with quotation marks rather than separate words.*** If you type *ski resort,* you could get results of (1) everything to do with skis on the one hand and (2) everything to do with resorts—winter, summer, mountain, seaside—on the other. Better to put your phrase in quotation marks—*"ski resort"*—to narrow your search.

- ***Put unique words first in a phrase.*** Better to have *"Tom Wolfe novels"* rather than *"Novels Tom Wolfe."* Or if you're looking for the Hoagy Carmichael song rather than the southern state, type *"Georgia on My Mind."*

- ***Use operators—AND, OR, NOT, and + and – signs.*** Most search sites use symbols called *Boolean operators* to make searching more precise. To illustrate how they are used, suppose you're looking for the song "Strawberry Fields Forever."[3]

  AND connects two or more search words and means that all of them must appear in the search results. *Example: Strawberry AND Fields AND Forever.*

  OR connects two or more search words and indicates that any of the two may appear in the results. *Example: Strawberry Fields OR Strawberry fields.*

  NOT, when inserted before a word, excludes that word from the results. *Example: Strawberry Fields NOT Sally NOT W.C.* (to distinguish from the actress Sally Fields and comedian W. C. Fields).

  + (plus sign), like *AND,* precedes a word that must appear: *Example: + Strawberry + Fields.*

  – (minus sign), like *NOT,* excludes the word that follows it. *Example: Strawberry Fields – Sally.*

- ***Read the Help or Search Tips section.*** All search sites provide a Help section and tips. This could save you time later.

- ***Try an alternate general search site or a specific search site.*** If you're looking for very specific information, a general type of search site such as Yahoo! or AltaVista may not be the best way to go. Instead you should turn to a specific search site. *Examples:* To explore public companies, try Company Sleuth (*www.companysleuth.com*), Hoover's Online (*www.hoovers.com*), or KnowX (*www.knowx.com*). For news stories, try Yahoo News (*dailynews. yahoo.com*) or TotalNews (*www.totalnews.com*). For pay-per-look information, try Dialog Web (*www.dialogweb.com*), Lexis-Nexis (*www.lexis-nexis. com*), and Dow Jones Interactive (*www.djnr.com*).

MULTIMEDIA ON THE WEB

Many Websites (especially those trying to sell you something) are multimedia, using a combination of text, images, sound, video, or animation. Although you may be satisfied with static text-only Web pages for now, eventually you'll probably want more. Following are tools you will need to access more complex Web media.

PLUG-INS AND HELPER APPLICATIONS   In the 1990s, as the Web was evolving from text to multimedia, browsers were unable to handle many kinds of graphic, sound, and video files. To do so, external application files called "plug-ins" had to be loaded into the system. A *__plug-in__*—**also called a "player" or a "viewer"—is a program that adds a specific feature to a browser, allowing it to play or view certain files.** For example, to view certain documents, you may need to download Adobe Acrobat Reader; to listen to CD-quality video, you may need to download Liquid MusicPlayer. Plug-ins are required by many Websites if you want to fully experience their content.

Recent versions of Microsoft Internet Explorer and Netscape Communicator can handle a lot of multimedia. Now, if you come across a file for which you need a plug-in or add-on, the browser will ask whether you want it, then tell you how to go about downloading it, usually at no charge.

DEVELOPING MULTIMEDIA: APPLETS, JAVA, JAVASCRIPT, AND ACTIVE X   How do Website developers get all those nifty special multimedia effects? Often Web pages contain links to *__applets__*, **small programs that can be quickly downloaded and run by most browsers.** Applets are written in *Java*, a complex programming language that enables programmers to create animated and interactive Web pages. Java applets enhance Web pages by playing music, displaying graphics and animation, and providing interactive games.

If you are creating your own Web multimedia, you may want to learn techniques, such as JavaScript and ActiveX, that may be used to create Web-page interest and activity—such as scrolling banners, pop-up menus, and the like.

TEXT AND IMAGES   You can call up all kinds of text documents on the Web, such as newspapers, magazines, famous speeches, and works of literature. You can also view images, such as scenery, famous paintings, and photographs. Most Web pages combine both text and images.

ANIMATION   *__Animation__* **is the rapid sequencing of still images to create the appearance of motion,** as in a Road Runner cartoon. Animation is used in online video games as well as in moving banners displaying sports scores or stock prices.

VIDEO   Video can be transmitted in two ways: (1) A file, such as a movie or video clip, may have to be completely downloaded before you can view it. This may take several minutes in some cases. (2) A file may be displayed as streaming video and viewed while it is still being downloaded to your computer. *__Streaming video__* **is the process of transferring data in a continuous flow so that you can begin viewing a file even before the end is sent.** For instance, RealPlayer offers live, television-style broadcasts over the Internet as streaming video for viewing on your PC screen. You download RealPlayer's software, install it, then point your browser to a site featuring RealVideo. That will produce a streaming-video television image in a window a few inches wide.

AUDIO   Audio, such as sound or music files, may also be transmitted in two ways: (1) files that must be downloaded completely before they can be played or (2) files that are ***streaming audio,*** **allowing you to listen to the file while the data are still being downloaded to your computer.** A popular standard for transmitting audio is RealAudio, which can compress sound so it can be played in real time, even though sent over telephone lines. You can, for instance, listen to 24-hour-a-day net.radio, which features "vintage rock," or English-language services of 19 shortwave outlets from World Radio Network in London. Many large radio stations outside the United States have net.radio, allowing people in foreign lands to listen to their home stations.

The Internet Telephone & Videophone

A few years ago, the idea of using the Internet to make phone calls was considered a gimmicky technology for nerdy hobbyists. Now Internet firms have taken aim at the traditional telephone companies.

The key element is that the Internet breaks up conversations (as it does any other transmitted data) into "information packets," which can be sent over separate lines, then regrouped at the destination, whereas conventional voice phone lines carry a conversation over a single path. Thus, the Internet can move a lot more traffic over a network than the traditional telephone link can.

With ***Internet telephony***—**using the Net to make phone calls, either one-to-one or for audioconferencing**—you can make long-distance phone calls that are surprisingly inexpensive. Indeed, it's theoretically possible to do this without owning a computer, simply by picking up your standard telephone and dialing a number that will "packetize" your conversation. However, it's more common practice to use a PC with a sound card and a microphone, a modem linked to a standard Internet service provider, and Internet telephone software such as Netscape Conference (part of Netscape Communicator) or Microsoft NetMeeting (part of Microsoft Internet Explorer).

Besides carrying voice signals, Internet telephone software also allows videoconferencing, enabling you and others to be linked by a videophone that will transmit pictures of the people in the conversation, assuming everyone has a video camera attached to their PC. It can also allow people to make sketches on "whiteboards" as they talk, as when three architecture students meet online to discuss the floor plan for a new house.

Designing Web Pages

If you want to have your own personal Website, you will need to design a Web page, determine any hyperlinks, and hire 24-hour-a-day space on a Web server or buy one of your own. Professional Web-page designers can produce a page for you, or you can do it yourself using a menu-driven program included with your Web browser or a Web-page design software package, such as Microsoft FrontPage or Adobe PageMill. After you have designed your Web page, you can put it on your ISP's server.

OTHER INTERNET RESOURCES: FTP, TELNET, NEWSGROUPS, & REAL-TIME CHAT

E-mail and the World Wide Web seem to attract all the attention. But other cyber resources are also widely used: FTP, Telnet, newsgroups, and real-time chat.

FTP: FOR COPYING ALL THE FREE FILES YOU WANT   Many Net users enjoy "FTPing"—cruising the system and checking into some of the tens of thousands of FTP sites, which predate the Web and offer interesting free files to copy (download). **_FTP_, for _file transfer protocol_, is a method whereby you can connect to a remote computer (called an "FTP site") and transfer publicly available files to your own microcomputer's hard disk.** The free files offered cover nearly anything that can be stored on a computer: software, games, photos, maps, art, music, books, statistics.

Some FTP files are open to the public, some are not. For instance, a university might maintain an FTP site with private files (such as lecture transcripts) available only to professors and students with assigned user names and passwords. It might also have public FTP files open to anyone with an e-mail address. You can download FTP files using either your Web browser or special software (called an _FTP client program_), such as Fetch.

TELNET: FOR CONNECTING TO REMOTE COMPUTERS   **_Telnet_ is a program or command that allows you to connect to remote computers on the Internet.** This feature, which allows microcomputers to communicate successfully with mainframes, enables you to tap into Internet computers and access public files as though you were connected directly instead of, for example, through your ISP site.

The Telnet feature is especially useful for perusing large databases at universities, government agencies, or libraries. As an electronic version of a library card catalog, Telnet can be used to search most major public and university library catalogs. (See, for example, Internet Public Library, _www.ipl.org_, and Library Spot, _www.libraryspot.com_)

NEWSGROUPS: FOR ONLINE TYPED DISCUSSIONS ON SPECIFIC TOPICS   **A _newsgroup_ is a giant electronic bulletin board on which users conduct written discussions about a specific subject.** There are more than 30,000 newsgroup forums—which charge no fee—and they cover an amazing array of topics. Examples are _www.tlpoe.com_, for oyster lovers, and _www.wdxcyber.com_, for discussions and information on women's health care. (For a small fee, services such as Maganet.news.com and Binaries.net will get you access to 50,000–90,000 newsgroups all over the world.)

Newsgroups take place on a special network of computers called **_Usenet_, a worldwide network of servers that can be accessed through the Internet.** To participate, you need a **_newsreader_, a program included with most browsers that allows you to access a newsgroup and read or type messages.** (Messages, incidentally, are known as *articles*.)

One way to find a newsgroup of interest to you is to use a portal such as Yahoo!, Excite, or Lycos to search Usenet for specific topics. Or you can use the search engine Google's Deja Usenet Archive (*http://groups.google.com/googlegroups/deja*), which will present the newsgroups matching the topic you specify. About a dozen major topics, identified by abbreviations ranging from *alt* (alternative topics) to *talk* (opinion and discussion), are divided into hierarchies of subtopics.

REAL-TIME CHAT: FOR TYPED DISCUSSIONS WHILE ONLINE AT THE SAME TIME   With newsgroups (and mailing lists, described under e-mail on page 28), participants may contribute to a discussion, then go away and return hours or days later to catch up on others' typed contributions. **With _real-time chat (RTC)_, participants have a typed discussion ("chat") while online at the same time,** just like a telephone conversation, except that messages are typed rather than spoken. Otherwise the format is much like a newsgroup, with a message board to which participants may send ("post") their contributions. To start a chat, you use what is known as a *chat client,* such as IRC (Internet Relay Chat)—a program available on your browser that will connect you to a chat server.

Unlike instant messaging (discussed on page 28), which tends to involve one-on-one conversation, real-time chat usually involves several participants. As a result, RTC "is often like being at a crowded party," says one writer. "There are any number of people present and many threads of conversation occurring all at once."[4]

Time Management

The Secret to Succeeding at Distance Learning

If you don't feel you're a terrific student or time manager, just fake it.

Seriously.

Even if you haven't done well in school in the past, pretend now that you're the ultimate student. Make as though you're a scholar. Play at being organized. Simulate being a good time manager.

There's a reason for all this: Chances are that, if you *act* like the person you want to become, you will *become* that person. This is true whether it's being less shy, having a more optimistic outlook, having more self-esteem, or being a better student. Once you've become used to your new role, the feelings of discomfort that "This isn't natural for me" will probably begin to go away. In many kinds of behavior change, *you are more apt to ACT your way into a new way of thinking than to THINK your way into it.*[1]

If you doubt that this works, just consider that people act their way into behavior change all the time. People may not feel as if they can handle the responsibilities of a promotion or a new job beforehand, but they usually do. Being a parent looks pretty awesome when you're holding a newborn baby, but most people in the world get used to it.

"If you want a quality, act as if you already had it," suggested psychologist William James. "Try the 'as if' technique." In other words: Fake it till you make it. In this chapter, we'll examine how to fake your way into managing your time.

GETTING REAL ABOUT STUDYING

You may have heard a fellow student say offhandedly, "Yeah, I got an A in the course. But I hardly had to study at all."

Don't believe it.

Sure, perhaps there really are some people who can get by this way (or courses that are really that easy). However, most people who talk like that just want to look as though they are so brainy that they don't need to study. In reality, either they are probably studying a lot or they are *not* getting top grades.

Here is clearly an area in which you have to bite the bullet. Quite often, studying is hard work. It *does* take time. Most students probably *don't* like to do it.

Learning can be fun, but studying *isn't* always something to look forward to. In short, studying may well be the first test of your ability to develop *staying power*— that is, persistence, commitment, discipline.

You need not feel upset or guilty about this. Accept that studying is not always something you're going to do because you feel like it. Then you can begin to organize your time so that you can always get enough studying done.

As your starting point, assume this near-universal equation:

STUDENTS ARE EXPECTED TO DEVOTE AT LEAST 2 HOURS OF STUDY FOR EVERY HOUR OF CLASS.

By "study," we mean reviewing notes, reading assignments, writing papers—all the activity known as homework. Some classes may require less than 2 hours, but some might require more. Indeed, some might require 3 or 4 hours of study for every hour in class, if you find the subject hard going.

THREE STEPS FOR IMPROVING YOUR TIME MANAGEMENT

Following are Steps 1–3 of the Essential Strategy for Time Management.

- **Step 1: "What is my master timetable?"** In this step you set your schedule for the semester or quarter.
- **Step 2: "What is my weekly timetable?"** This is the schedule you follow from week to week.
- **Step 3: "What is on the to-do list today?"** This errand list (or "things-to-do" list) is no different from the to-do list that millions of people make every day.

Step 1: What Is My Master Timetable?

To make a master timetable for the semester or quarter, do the following:

- **Obtain a month-at-a-glance calendar with lots of writing room.** This calendar should cover all the weeks in the school term. It should have big squares for all the days of the month, squares large enough to write five to ten words in. When filled in with due dates and appointments, this will become your master timetable for the semester or quarter.
- **Obtain your institution's academic calendar.** If your distance learning course is being offered through a school (rather than, say, a corporate training department), you need to obtain the institution's academic calendar (either printed in the school's catalog or available online at its Website). The academic calendar tells you school holidays, registration dates, and deadlines for meeting various academic requirements. It usually also indicates when final exam week takes place.
- **Obtain the course outline for each course.** As we mentioned in Chapter 1, **the course outline or course information sheet, known as the <u>syllabus</u> ("*sil*-uh-bus"), tells you midterm and final exam dates, quiz**

dates (if any), and due dates for term papers or projects. The syllabus is given to you by your instructor, either mailed to you in a course packet or posted online.

Now go through the school calendar and all your course outlines. Transfer to your master timetable calendar all class tests, important dates, and deadlines. These include pertinent due dates, dates for the beginning and end of the term, and school holidays. Note any online discussion times and dates that are scheduled. Also add other dates and hours you know about. Examples are those for job, medical and dental appointments, concerts, sports events, and birthdays. Leave enough space for any given day so that you can add other entries later, if necessary.

Note: Consider using a different, highly visible color—flaming red, say—to record critical items such as test dates.

To begin making up your own master timetable for the present semester or quarter, use a blank calendar. After it is completed, you can three-hole punch it and put it in your binder or notebook. Or you can post it on the wall above the place where you usually study.

Step 2: What Is My Weekly Timetable?

The main point of creating a weekly timetable is to schedule your study time.

Some students aren't sure what is meant by "study time." They think of it as something they do a day or two before a test. *By study time we mean everything connected to the process of learning.* This means preparing for tests, certainly, but also reading textbook chapters and other required readings, researching and writing papers, doing projects, and so on. Studying is *homework,* and it's an ongoing process.

By actually creating a weekly timetable to schedule their study time, students put themselves on notice that they take their studying seriously. They tell themselves their study time is as important as their classes, job, family meals, or other activities with fixed times. It is a visible expression of their persistence.

If you don't schedule your study time, you may well study only when something else isn't going on. Or you will study late at night, when your energy level is down. Or you will postpone studying until the night before a test—all bad ideas.

The weekly master plan should include those activities that happen at fixed, predictable times. These are your classes, work, regularly scheduled student or family activities—and your regularly scheduled studying times. As mentioned, study time should amount to about 2 hours of studying for every hour of class time, perhaps more. For online courses that don't have scheduled blocks of classes, you will find that you need to spend not only a great deal of time online (engaging in reading and discussions) but also off line (reading textbooks and other assignments).

If you want, you can add meals, exercise, and commuting or transportation times. However, we believe that the fewer things you have on your calendar, the more you'll pay attention to the things that are there. Otherwise, you may start feeling overregulated. You shouldn't schedule break times, for instance; you'll be able to judge for yourself the best times to stop for a breather. (We describe extended study time and breaks on page 50.)

Make up your own weekly timetable for this semester or quarter, indicating your recurring responsibilities every week in this term. This, too, may be three-hole punched and placed in your notebook or prominently posted near your principal study place.

Step 3: What Is on the To-Do List Today?

The final step is just like the informal to-do lists that many people have, whether students or nonstudents.

The to-do list can be made up every week or every evening, after referring to your master timetable and weekly timetable. It can be done on a notepad or a 3″ × 5″ card. Either way, it should be easy to carry around so that you can cross things off or make additions. You can be as general or as detailed as you want with this piece of paper, but the main purpose of a to-do list is twofold:

- **Reminders:** Remind yourself to do things you might otherwise forget. Examples are doctor's appointments, things to shop for, and books to return to the library. Don't forget to write down promises you made to people (such as to get them a phone number or a photocopy of your class notes).
- **Priorities:** Set priorities for what you will do with your day. It may be unnecessary to list your scheduled classes, because you will probably go to them anyway. If you're in an online class without a scheduled meeting time, remind yourself to log on (perhaps every day) to the course Website and participate in any activities, such as discussions.

  You might also want to list an hour or half-hour for exercise, if you're planning on it. You may wish to list laundry, shopping, and so on. However, *the most important thing you can do is to set priorities for what you're going to study that day.* Thus, your to-do list should have items such as "Tues.— Read math chapter 13" and "Wed. P.M.—Start library research for Business Communication paper."

Most managers and administrators find a to-do list essential to avoid being overwhelmed by the information overload of their jobs. Since you, too, are on the verge of drowning in information and deadlines, you'll no doubt find the to-do list a helpful tool. Clearly also the to-do list is another application that you can carry over from your educational experience to the world outside of school.

On a separate piece of paper, make up your own to-do list for tomorrow.

BATTLING THE KILLER TIME WASTERS

Even if you had 25 hours in a day, could you manage the time any more efficiently? What about 26 or 27 hours?

Everyone gets the same ration, a disappointingly small 24 hours a day. Although some people are indeed smarter, usually the ones who excel at school and at work simply use their time better. If you try the Self-Analysis on the next page for a week, you can begin to see where your time goes.

Self-Analysis: How Do You Spend Your Time?

The purpose of this activity is to enable you to see where your time goes. Honesty is important. The idea is to figure out how much time you do spend on studying. Then you can determine if you could spend *more* time.

Keeping a Log of Your Time: Record how many hours you spend each day on the following activities. (There are 168 hours in a week.)

	MON	TUES	WED	THUR	FRI	SAT	SUN
1. Sleeping							
2. Showering, dressing, and so on							
3. Eating							
4. Traveling to and from work and other places							
5. Going to classes							
6. Working							
7. Watching television							
8. Important after-work or after-school activities (e.g., child care, sports)							
9. Other leisure activities (e.g., movies, parties, hanging out)							
10. Other scheduled matters— church, tutoring, volunteering							
11. Studying							
Total hours							

Your Interpretation: We put "Studying" at the bottom of the list so you can see how other activities in your life impinge on it.

Now consider the following:

1. Do you feel you are in control of your time? _____
2. Are you satisfied with the way you spend your time? _____
3. On what three activities do you spend the most time?

   _____

   _____

   _____

4. Do you feel you're giving enough time to studying? _____
5. If you had to give more time to studying, what two or three activities could you give up or cut down on?

   _____

   _____

   _____

How You Spend Your Time

You have 168 hours in a week (7 days of 24 hours each). Let's see where the time is apt to go.

- *Sleeping:* Everyone needs between 6 and 9 hours of sleep a night. If you short yourself on sleep, you may find the "sleep deficit" causes you to doze off in class. But it's possible you may be able to make it up by, for example, napping on the bus.
- *Showering, dressing, grooming:* This might take 30–60 minutes a day. It depends on how long you shower, whether you shave, if you put on makeup at home or on the bus, and so on.
- *Meals, family responsibilities:* Eating might take at least an hour a day, perhaps 14–21 hours in a week. If you skip breakfast and even lunch, you still probably have at least a snack or two throughout the day. Dinner might just be a quick visit to Burger King or microwaving a prefab dinner pulled from the freezer. Or it might mean shopping for, preparing, cooking, eating, and cleaning up after a full-scale meal for your family (and making lunches for others for the next day). In any case, you'd be surprised the amount of time eating takes out of your week. And other family responsibilities, such as child care, can really add up.
- *Commuting, travel time, errands:* Travel time—between home and job, and so on—might take an hour or more a day, perhaps 10–16 hours a week. In recent times, the average commute to work by car has been found to be 10.4 miles and 19.7 minutes. In some areas, travel may take much longer.[2]

  When computing travel time, remember to include waiting at bus or subway stops, looking for parking places, and walking from bus stop or car to classes. You also have to total all the time involved in getting yourself not only to job and home but also, for example, in picking up children from day care, shopping, and running errands.
- *Classes and work:* Figuring out the amount of time you spend in class—whether DL or walk-in—is easy. If you're enrolled in three courses, totaling 9 credit hours, you should be spending 9 hours a week in class.

  If you work while going to school, you can probably easily figure out the hours your job requires each week. (Two exceptions are if you're subject to unpredictable overtime hours or if you're working for a temporary-employment agency.)

  Incidentally, time researchers John P. Robinson and Geoffrey Godbey, authors of *Time for Life,* have found that, despite everyone's notion that they are overworked, the average work week has shrunk since 1965—about 6 hours less for working women and about 7 hours less for working men.[3]
- *Television:* Television, it turns out, takes up an enormous amount of most people's time. We discuss this below, under "The Really Big Time Wasters" on page 55.
- *Studying:* As mentioned, on average you should devote 2 hours of studying outside class for every hour you are in class. With three courses requiring 9 hours a week in the classroom, for example, you should be spending 18 hours a week doing homework.

Add up the hours in these categories for the week, then subtract them from 168. What's left over is the time you have left for everything else. This means *EVERYTHING*: hanging out, parties, sports, playing with or helping children, doing household chores (if not included above), religious activities, and so on.

Does it seem, then, that you're suddenly going to have to be more efficient about how you manage your time? What follows are some suggestions for battling the killer time wasters.

Schedule Study Sessions That Actually Work

As we've said, creating a schedule for studying *and sticking with it* are terribly important. Indeed, this is probably the single most valuable piece of advice anyone can give you.

There are, however, certain things to consider when you sit down to block out the master timetable that includes your study time:

- *Make study times during your best time of day.* Are you a morning person or a night person? That is, are you most alert before breakfast or most able to concentrate in the evening when it's quiet? When possible, schedule some of your study time for the times of day when you do your best work. These are particularly good times for doing difficult assignments, such as writing research papers.
- *Don't schedule overly long sessions.* Imagine how you're going to feel at the start of a day in which you've scheduled 10 hours for studying. You'll probably take your time getting to work and won't do more than 7–9 hours of actual studying that day anyway.

  To avoid setting yourself up for failure, we suggest programming no more than 4–6 hours of studying in a day. Also, divide that time block into two 2- or 3-hour sessions separated by perhaps a couple of hours of time off. (Actually, many students will find they just can't stand 6 hours of studying in a single day.) And if you do schedule long blocks of study time, mix the subjects you're working on so you'll have some variety. The point, after all, is not *how long* you study but *how effectively* you study.

  Perhaps an even better strategy, however, is to schedule several short sessions rather than a handful of long sessions. We find, for instance, that we perform much better when we have several short stints of work rather than one long one.
- *Allow for 5- to 10-minute study breaks.* Some people are like long-distance runners and do better by studying for long sessions—for example, 50 minutes followed by a 10-minute break. Others are like sprinters and perform better by studying for 25 minutes followed by a 5-minute break.

  Of course, you don't have to go exactly by the clock, but you should definitely permit yourself frequent, regularly scheduled breaks. Taken at regular intervals, breaks actually produce efficiencies. They enable you to concentrate better while studying, reduce fatigue, motivate you to keep going, and allow material to sink in while you're resting.

Breaks should be small ways of *entertaining yourself*—going for a soft drink, taking a walk outside, glancing through a newspaper. We don't recommend getting on the phone, picking up your guitar, or dropping in on a friend, however, unless you can keep it short. You don't want the diversion to be so good that it wrecks your study routine.

- ***Reward yourself when you're done studying.*** The end of the course is weeks away, the attainment of a degree months or years. What's going to keep you going in the meantime?

    You need to give yourself as many immediate rewards as you can for studying, things to look forward to when you finish. Examples are a snack, phone talk with a friend, some music or TV time. Parts of your DL experience may be a grind, but you don't want it to be *just* a grind. Rewards are important.

If, after scheduling in your study time, you find it still isn't enough, you need to see where you can make adjustments. Can you reduce the number of courses? Work fewer hours? Get help with chores from family members? Whatever, the main thing is to make your scheduled study time effective when you're doing it.

Fight Distractions!

A phone call comes in while you're studying, and 20 minutes later you finish the conversation. Are you later going to tell yourself that you actually studied during your scheduled study time? Or are you going to pretend that you'll simply make up the work some other time?

Such interruptions may be common, but it's important that you not lie to yourself—that you not play games with your study time. The following are some strategies for preventing or handling common distractions:

- ***Establish a couple of places where all you do is study.*** On campus, you see students studying just about everywhere, which is fine. Distance learners may study at home, at work during breaks, on a bus or train, or other places. Whatever, it's important that you establish a couple of places for regular studying and, if possible, do nothing else there. Unless you can't avoid it, don't routinely study on your bed, where you might fall asleep. Don't work in front of the TV. If you use your study places only for studying, they will become associated just with that and will reinforce good study behavior.[4]
- ***Establish a good study environment.*** For your principal study site, the best arrangement is a separate room, such as a spare room, that you treat as your home office. Otherwise, use a corner of your bedroom or dormitory room. Turn a desk or table to the wall to provide yourself with as much privacy as possible from others sharing the room. Make an agreement with your family that your study space is off limits to them.

    Make this spot as comfortable and organized as you can. Make sure you have the right temperature, good lighting, and a comfortable chair. The desk should have room for a computer or a typewriter, as well as reading and writing space. Books and supplies should be within reach. Having a personal-ized bulletin board is useful. Post important information, such as calendars, schedules, and announcements, on the wall nearby. (You can also post motivational slogans—"EDUCATION: ONE ASSIGNMENT AT A TIME!"—and notes nearby.)

Adult returning students in particular may have to be somewhat asser-tive with others in their household about their need for a quiet space. Sometimes having a "noise machine," such as an air purifier or electronic white-noise machine, can mask distracting sounds and help you concentrate better.

- *Fight electronic distractions.* Electronic equipment has completely taken over many households and residences. It has also taken over many student residence halls. One college administrator says that "the walls in some students' rooms look like the flight deck of the space shuttle."[5] If you're taking an online course, be mindful that the constant distractions of the Internet will be very close at hand.

  If the noise becomes too overwhelming and you can't get it turned down by common agreement, go somewhere else. Plan to do your studying in a quiet place—even a storage or laundry room.

- *Avoid "multitasking."* Nearly four-fifths of Internet users who spend 5 hours or more a week online do "multitasking"—that is, they engage in another activity while online: eating and drinking, listening to the radio, watching TV, talking on the phone, or chatting with others in the room.[6] But, experts say, just because we *can* do everything doesn't mean we have to—or should.[7]

  Studies show that trying to do two or more mentally demanding tasks—such as homework and something else—is actually self-defeating, burning up more total brainpower than if you did them one at a time. And research also suggests that people are becoming less happy and more error-prone in the process. "From university centers to federal aviation labs," says one account, "studies show that people can juggle a fair number of tasks—and even get better at this by picking what balls they toss in the air. But often, dividing their attention makes them exhausted, stressed, and more forgetful."[8]

  It may seem cool to have a lot of electronic gadgets—TV, VCR, CD player, personal computer, handheld computer, pager, cellphone, fax ma-chine, and so on. But what do we need? "Which machines really serve you?" asks productivity specialist Odette Pollar. "Adjust your attitude to all this abundance by making sure these machines conform to your pace."[9]

  Of course, if you're a single parent juggling school, work, and children, you may be forced to deal with multiple tasks all the time. The chances are you'll be able to handle them. But be aware that constant interruptions can kill your concentration if you're trying to study.

- *Fight telephone distractions.* Of course you don't have to make any outgoing calls during your scheduled study times, and you should resist doing so. As for incoming calls, there are four things you can do: (1) Be disciplined and don't answer the phone at all. (2) Answer the phone, but tell the caller you'll have to call back because "I'm studying for an important course right now." (3) Tell whoever answers the phone to take a message for you. (4) Let an answering machine or voice-mail system collect your calls, then call back later.

- *Fight people distractions.* People interruptions can be a real problem, and eventually you have to learn to "just say no." Avoid being complaining or accusatory, but do be polite and direct. *Don't complain, don't explain, just declare.* So when interrupted, you just declare: "Jackie, this is interesting, but I have to study right now. Let's talk later."

  Early on you need to develop some understanding with your housemates or family members about your study requirements. Show them your study schedule. Tell them when you're at your desk, you're supposed to be doing your schoolwork. Ask them for their assistance in helping you to accomplish this. One writer says that a student he knows always wears a colorful hat when he wants to study. "When his wife and children see the hat, they respect his wish to be left alone."[10]

  What if you're a parent and have nowhere to put a young child (not even in front of a television set or in a room full of toys)? In that case, just plan on doing the kind of studying that is not too demanding, expecting to be interrupted. Or use your study breaks to play with the child. Or take a few minutes to play attentively with the child before you hit the books, then say you have work to do. Or even read your textbook aloud to the child, making it sound interesting (a tactic that will probably last as long as the child's attention span). As long as the child feels he or she is getting some of your attention, you can still get some things done. Most adult DL students with children tell us they do a great deal of studying after the kids are asleep.

Of course, you can't control everything. Things will come up that will cut into your study time, as in the electricity going off or the flu wiping you out. That's why it's important to think of your scheduled study sessions as practically sacred.

Fight Delaying Tactics!

All of us put off doing things sometimes. Delaying tactics can result when your prospective task is boring, long, or difficult. You need to look hard to see if one of these reasons applies, then fight back by applying the appropriate strategies:

- *Fight boring assignments with short concentrations of effort.* If the task is boring, you need to concentrate on seeing how fast you can get a portion of it done. That is, you need to concentrate on the benefits of completing it in a short time rather than on the character of the task itself.

  Thus, you can say to yourself, "I'm going to work on this for 15 minutes without stopping, applying my full concentration. Then I'm going to move along to something else." You can stand anything for 15 minutes, right? And this task may seem more acceptable if it's not seen as several hours of work—especially if you plan a little reward for yourself (getting a soft drink, say) at the end of that time.

- *Fight long assignments by breaking them into smaller tasks.* Most people have a difficult time tackling large projects, such as research papers. Indeed, most of us tend to take on simple, routine tasks first, saving the longer ones for later when we'll supposedly "have more time."[11] Thus, we often delay beginning large assignments so long that we can't do an effective job when we finally do turn to them.

  The way to avoid this difficulty is to break the large assignments into smaller tasks. You then schedule each of these tasks individually over several days or weeks. (That's how this book got written—in small amounts over several weeks.) For example, when reading a chapter on a difficult subject, read just five or seven pages at a time.

- *Fight difficult tasks by tackling them first and making sure you understand them.* If you have one particular area of study that's difficult or unpleasant, *do that one first,* when your energy level is higher and you can concentrate best. For instance, if you find math problems or language learning more difficult than reading a psychology text, tackle them first. The easiest tasks, such as list making and copying chores, can be done late in the day when you're tired.

  If a task seems difficult, you may also take it as a warning signal: Maybe there's something about it you don't understand. Are the directions clear? Is the material over your head? If either of these conditions is true, *run, do not walk,* to your instructor. Ask for clarification, if directions are the problem. Be frank with the instructor if you think the material (statistics? grammar? lab experiments?) is hard to comprehend or perform. It may be that what you need is to quickly get yourself the help of a tutor.

  We can't stress enough the importance of taking your own worries seriously if you find that what you're studying is too difficult. However, if you can deal with this before the school term is too far along, you'll probably be all right.

Fight Procrastination & Other Negative Reactions!

Delaying tactics generally occur unintentionally or only occasionally. **_Procrastination_, on the other hand, is defined as putting off things intentionally and habitually.**

Although it's tempting to think of procrastinators as people who are disorganized or lazy, this is not the case, according to psychologist Linda Sapadin, author of *It's About Time.*[12] There are six styles of procrastinators, Sapadin says: perfectionists, dreamers, worriers, crisis makers, defiers, and overdoers.[13] Time-management tips, she says, won't help. Rather, what's required is that procrastinators understand the emotional problems that are hobbling them, then work to change the thinking behind them. If you don't understand why you delay time after time and always feel recurring regret but aren't confident you can change—an erroneous presumption—you need to consider this angle.

Procrastination is only one kind of emotional response to task avoidance. There are, however, several other reasons why students may blow an assignment or a course because something about it is emotionally disagreeable or frightening.

Maybe, for instance, it's some aspect of shyness, so that you find making a presentation—even an online presentation—nearly unbearable. (Shyness, incidentally, is an extremely common condition, one afflicting 4 out of 10 people.[14]) Maybe it's some deep embarrassment about your writing or language skills. Maybe you think, "I'm no good at math." Maybe you find working online an alien experience. Maybe there's a former boyfriend or girlfriend in the class whose presence is upsetting you. Maybe the instructor turns you off in some way.

These and most similar situations can be helped, but *you have to reach out and get the help*. If you don't feel you can take the problem up with your instructor, then *immediately* contact your academic adviser, if you have one. If you have access to the school's campus, go to the student counseling center. Some schools now offer counseling and tutoring online as well. In any event, try not to wait until you're overwhelmed.

THE REALLY BIG TIME WASTERS

There are a handful of areas that will, if you allow them to, take vast tracts of time, putting studying in serious jeopardy. They are *television watching, partying, Internet addiction,* and *unnecessary work.*

TELEVISION WATCHING   TV, say Robinson and Godbey, is "the 800-pound gorilla of free time."[15]

Since 1965, these sociologists have asked thousands of people to keep hour-by-hour diary accounts of what they do and for how long, from the time they wake up to the time they go to sleep. In the 32 years since their study began, they found that television has gobbled up ever more free time. In 1997 women watched 14.5 hours a week (up from 9.3 in 1965). Men watched 15.8 hours (up from 11.3).

Television is such an ingrained habit, says Robinson, that "people say they don't have any time because they're watching television. It's like some sort of . . . alien force out there, over which they have no control."

Paradoxically, although we spend far more time watching television than any other leisure activity (including reading books or magazines or listening to music), Americans report in surveys that TV is one of the first activities they would give up if they had to. Is this something you feel you could do?

If you're watching the standard 15 hours of television a week, that's equivalent to the time it's recommended you spend on a course that meets 5 hours a week (one 5-credit course)—both class and homework time.

PARTYING   As a distance learning student, you may not have much to do with school social life. You may be aware, however, that drinking is a big fact of life on a lot of college campuses. "Partying starts on Thursday nights" and continues through the weekend, wrote a recent graduate of one major eastern university. He went on to explain: "You must understand that partying and getting drunk are synonymous to a college student."[16] People in general—and college students in particular—tend to equate drinking alcohol with relaxation, good times, fellowship, and the easing of pain and problems. More than a third of first-year students, however, drink simply to get drunk.

Campus drinking is said to be less than it used to be.[17] Nevertheless, a Harvard University study of 17,592 students on 140 campuses reported that 50 percent of male college students and 39 percent of female students were binge drinkers. ***Binge drinking* is defined as consuming five (for men) or four (for women) or more drinks in a row one or more times in a two-week period.**[18] Among the results of heavy drinking: (1) Nearly two-thirds of binge drinkers reported having missed a class. (2) Students with D or F grade averages drink, on average, three times as much (nearly 11 drinks a week) as A students (3.4 drinks a week).[19]

INTERNET ADDICTION   Don't let this happen to you: "A student e-mails friends, browses the World Wide Web, blows off homework, botches exams, flunks out of school."[20] This is a description of the downward spiral of the Net addict, often a college student—because schools give students no-cost or low-cost linkage to the Internet—though it can be anyone. Some become addicted (although critics feel "addiction" is too strong a word) to chat groups, some to online pornography, some simply to the escape from real life.[21]

Stella Yu, 21, a college student from Carson, California, was rising at 5 A.M. to get a few hours online before school, logging on to the Internet between classes and during her part-time job, and then going home to Web surf until 1 A.M. Her grades dropped and her father was irate over her phone bills, some as high as $450: "I always make promises I'm going to quit; that I'll just do it for research. But I don't. I use it for research for 10 minutes, then I spend two hours chatting."[22]

Yu stopped short of calling herself an Internet addict. A case of denial?

College students are unusually vulnerable to Internet addiction, which is defined as "a psychological dependence on the Internet, regardless of type of activity once 'logged on,'" according to psychologist Jonathan Kandell.[23] The American Psychological Association, which officially recognized pathological Internet use as a disorder in 1997, defines an ***Internet addict* as one who spends an average of 38 hours a week online.**[24] (The average Internet user spends 5½ hours a week on the activity.)

What are the consequences of Internet addiction disorder? A study of the first-year dropout rate at Alfred University in New York found that nearly half the students who quit the preceding semester had been engaging in marathon, late-night sessions on the Internet.[26] The University of California at Berkeley found some students linked to excessive computer use neglected their course work.[27] A survey by Viktor Brenner of State University of New York at Buffalo found that some Internet addicts had "gotten into hot water" with their school for Internet-related activities.[28]

THE COMMUTER RAT RACE   A good reason for taking a course by distance learning is that you avoid the time-consuming hassle of commuting. Still, 80 percent of college students are commuters. Some take public transportation, but others come by car.[29]

Commuting by car can be a wearing, time-consuming experience, especially during rush hour. "For those of you who do not know the commute pain, imagine sitting in bumper-to-bumper traffic, sucking up exhaust from cars and double-trailer trucks, watching out for lane jumpers and going only 10 miles in 30 minutes. Then imagine your commute is only one-third complete."

So writes a California man whose job changed from off hours to regular hours and as a result turned his 30-mile drive to work from 30 minutes to 90 minutes—one-way. Before the change, "I never had to go from 70 mph to a dead stop on the freeway every work day." He continues, "And then inch along and stop and inch along and stop and inch along and stop." [30]

Commuting by bus, train, or subway can also consume a great deal of time. Although public transportation may be advantageous if you can study during that time, the use of public transit, particularly of bus service, is declining throughout the United States. Thus, most people commute by car, usually alone, sometimes spending an hour or more every day.

Still, if you're a commuter, the question you have to ask yourself is: Is a car an absolute must? Often people think they need a car, but they really don't. For many people, particularly young people, it may really come down "to the difference between want and need," says one psychologist. "You would very much like to have a car: for independence, for status, and for the sense of power you feel when you drive," she says. "But you don't need one."[31]

Adds another writer, our dependence on a car "often has more to do with our lack of imagination and willingness to be flexible than it does on any real necessity." Indeed, he says, a simple shift in attitude—learning to view a car as a luxury rather than as a necessity—can save you a great deal of money.[32]

WORKING TOO MANY HOURS WHILE IN SCHOOL   While pursuing an undergraduate college degree, 8 out of 10 students work, and they are of two types: "employees who study, and students who work," says Jacqueline King of the American Council on Education.[33]

Full-time employees who also go to college make up about a third of working undergraduates. They are usually older and attend part-time.

The other two-thirds of working undergraduates are students who have jobs to meet college expenses. They are usually full-time students, under 24, and financially dependent on their parents. On average they work 25 hours a week. Often they are working because they want to lessen the need for student loans.

Working more than 15 hours a week can have a negative effect on students' chances of staying in school, according to a U.S. Department of Education study.[34] When full-time students work more than that, the competing demands can have unfortunate results. "Stressed-out students too often turn to drugs or binge drinking to 'blow off steam,'" says King, "with negative consequences for individual students as well as others on campus."[35]

One reason that students work too many hours is that they are trying to avoid borrowing for college expenses. According to a study by the U.S. Department of Education of students at public four-year institutions in a recent year:

1. 20 percent didn't take out loans and didn't work.
2. 15 percent took out loans, didn't work, or worked under 15 hours per week.
3. 40 percent didn't take out loans and worked 15 hours or more.
4. 25 percent took out loans and worked 15 hours or more.[36]

The best positions to be in, clearly, are 1 and 2. Borrowing money, incidentally, "does not seem to harm students' persistence in college or their academic success," King says. Better, then, to leave college owing some money than to work more than 15 hours a week and have no time left to really concentrate on your schoolwork.[37]

Maybe you can't do as much as you'd like about commuting and working while going to school. But you can decide not to be mindless about how you approach these matters.

GIVING YOURSELF THE EXTRA EDGE: DEVELOPING STAYING POWER IN YOUR STUDYING

We often read of the superstar athlete who spends many extra hours shooting baskets or sinking putts. Or we hear of the superstar performer who endlessly rehearses a song or an acting part. These people don't have The Extra Edge just because of talent. (There's *lots* of talent around, but few superstars.) They have put in the additional hours because they are in a highly competitive business and they want to perfect their craft. DL students are in the same situation.

What do you think when you see college or high school students studying on the campus lawn or in a bookstore line or at the bus stop? Perhaps you could think of them as doing just what the superstar basketball player shooting extra hoops does. *They are making use of the time-spaces in their day to gain The Extra Edge.* This, of course, is another variation on *exercising staying power.*

Following are some techniques that can boost your performance:

ALWAYS CARRY SOME SCHOOLWORK AND USE WAITING TIME
Your day is made up of intervals that can be used—waiting for meals, waiting for the bus, waiting for appointments. These 5- or 10- or 20-minute periods can add up to a lot of time during the day. The temptation is to use this time just to "space out" or to read a newspaper. There's nothing wrong with this kind of activity if you're trying to recharge your batteries in the midst of a stressful day—some mindlessness is allowable. However, these small bits of time can also be used to look over class notes, do some course-related reading, review reading notes, or read printouts of material from the online part of your course.

One other thing you can do is make a point of carrying 3″ × 5″ cards. These cards can contain important facts, names, definitions, formulas, and lists that you can pull out and memorize. Students learning a foreign language often carry flash cards, with foreign words on one side and the English meaning on the other. ***Flash cards* are cards bearing words, numbers, or pictures that are briefly displayed as a learning aid. One side of the card asks a question, the other side provides the answer.** Flash cards are also sold in bookstores for other subjects, such as biology, to help you learn definitions. You can make up flash cards of your own for many courses.

The 5-minute ministudy session is far more valuable than it might first seem. The way to better memorizing is simply to *practice practice practice*, or *rehearse rehearse rehearse.* Just as the superstars do.

USE YOUR SPARE TIME FOR THINKING   What do you think about when you're jogging, walking to work, standing in a bank line, inching along in traffic? It could be about anything, of course. (Many people think about relationships or sex.) However, you can make your mind more productive in three ways:

1. Try to recall points in a lecture that day.
2. Try to recall points in something you've read.
3. Think of ideas to go into a project or paper you're working on.

Again, the point of this use of idle time is to try to involve yourself with your schoolwork. This is equivalent to football players working plays in their heads or singers doing different kinds of phrasing in their minds. The superstars are always practicing, always working at their jobs.

JOIN A STUDY GROUP   Some students find that it helps to get together with a friend in the same course to study boring or difficult subjects. By exchanging ideas about the subject matter, you may find the time goes faster. Indeed, an extremely valuable aid to learning is the ***study group*, in which a group of classmates get together to share notes and ideas.** In a study group you can clarify lecture notes, quiz each other about ideas, and get different points of view about an instructor's objectives. Being in a group also helps to raise everyone's morale. It makes you realize that you are not alone. A study group can be face-to-face, on the telephone, or online.

MAKE TAPES OF LECTURES AND LISTEN TO THEM   This advice is particularly suitable for commuters with a tape deck in the car or those with a portable tape player who ride the bus. At the end of a long day, you might just want to space out to music. But what about at the beginning of the day, when you're fresh? That's the time for practicing some mindful behavior.

Making tapes of lectures, such as those given on live broadcast videos, is no substitute for taking notes. But listening to the tapes can provide you with *additional reinforcement*—especially important if the lecture is densely packed with information, as, say, a history or biology lecture might be.

Similarly, printing out text-based online lectures is much easier than reading them on screen.

Note: Be sure to ask your instructors for permission to tape them. Some institutions, in fact, *require* that you get the permission of instructors. At other schools, however, students are assumed to have the right to tape any instructor during class.

REVIEW NOTES ON A LAPTOP COMPUTER   If you use a portable computer to take notes of lectures and readings, then while you're waiting for the bus you can turn on your laptop and scroll through the notes you've made during the day.

Learning Strategies for Distance Learners

CHAPTER
4

Educators talk about differences in ***learning styles***—**the ways in which people acquire knowledge.** Some students learn well by listening to real-time lectures. Others learn better through reading, class discussion, hands-on experience, or researching a topic and writing about it. Thus, your particular learning style may make you more comfortable with some forms of teaching and learning, and even with some kinds of subjects, than with others.

Four Types of Learning Styles: Which Fits You?

To find out the ways you learn best, try the Self-Analysis exercise in the box below.

Self-Analysis: How Do You Learn Best?

There are 12 incomplete sentences and 3 choices for completing each. Circle the answer that best corresponds to your style, as follows:

> 1 = the choice that is *least* like you
> 2 = your second choice
> 3 = the choice that is *most* like you

1. When I want to learn something new, I usually . . .
   a. want someone to explain it to me. 1 2 3
   b. want to read about it in a book or magazine. 1 2 3
   c. want to try it out, take notes, or make a model of it. 1 2 3
2. At a party, most of the time I like to . . .
   a. listen and talk to two or three people at once. 1 2 3
   b. see how everyone looks and watch the people. 1 2 3
   c. dance, play games, or take part in some activities. 1 2 3
3. If I were helping with a musical show, I would most likely . . .
   a. write the music, sing the songs, or play the accompaniment. 1 2 3
   b. design the costumes, paint the scenery, or work the lighting effects. 1 2 3
   c. make the costumes, build the sets, or take an acting role. 1 2 3

---

4. When I am angry, my first reaction is to . . .
   a. tell people off, laugh, joke, or talk it over with someone. 1 2 3
   b. blame myself or someone else, daydream about taking revenge,
      or keep it inside. 1 2 3
   c. make a fist or tense my muscles, take it out on something else,
      hit or throw things. 1 2 3
5. A happy event I would like to have is . . .
   a. hearing the thunderous applause for my speech or music. 1 2 3
   b. photographing the prize picture of an exciting newspaper story. 1 2 3
   c. achieving the fame of being first in a physical activity such as
      dancing, acting, surfing, or sports event. 1 2 3
6. I prefer a teacher to . . .
   a. use the lecture method, with informative explanations
      and discussions. 1 2 3
   b. write on the chalkboard and use visual aids and assigned readings. 1 2 3
   c. require posters, models, or in-service practice and some activities
      in class. 1 2 3
7. I know that I talk with . . .
   a. different tones of voice. 1 2 3
   b. my eyes and facial expressions. 1 2 3
   c. my hands and gestures. 1 2 3
8. If I had to remember an event so I could record it later,
   I would choose to . . .
   a. tell it aloud to someone or hear an audiotape recording or
      a song about it. 1 2 3
   b. see pictures of it or read a description. 1 2 3
   c. replay it in some practice rehearsal, using movements such
      as dance, play acting, or drill. 1 2 3
9. When I cook something new, I like to . . .
   a. have someone tell me the directions, such as a friend or TV show. 1 2 3
   b. read the recipe and judge by how it looks. 1 2 3
   c. use many pots and dishes, stir often, and taste-test. 1 2 3
10. My emotions can often be interpreted from my . . .
   a. voice quality. 1 2 3
   b. facial expression. 1 2 3
   c. general body tone. 1 2 3
11. When driving, I . . .
   a. turn on the radio as soon as I enter the car. 1 2 3
   b. like quiet so I can concentrate. 1 2 3
   c. shift my body position frequently to avoid getting tired. 1 2 3
12. In my free time, I like to . . .
   a. listen to the radio, talk on the telephone, or attend a musical event. 1 2 3
   b. go to the movies, watch TV, or read a magazine or book. 1 2 3
   c. get some exercise, go for a walk, play games, or make things. 1 2 3

Scoring Add up the points for all the a's, then all the b's, then all the c's.
Total points for all a's: _____
Total points for all b's: _____
Total points for all c's: _____

(continued)

Self-Analysis: How Do You Learn Best? (continued)

Interpretation

If a has the highest score, that indicates your learning style preference is principally auditory.

If b has the highest score, your learning style preference is principally visual.

If c has the highest score, your learning style preference is kinesthetic.

If all scores are reasonably equal, that indicates your learning style preference is mixed. See the text for explanations.

Source: A. Ducharme and L. Watford, *Explanation of Assessment Area* [handout]. Reprinted with kind permission of Dr. Adele Ducharme and Dr. Luck Watford, Valdosta State University.

There are four ways in which people can learn new material: auditory, visual, kinesthetic, and mixed. Let's consider these.

AUDITORY LEARNING STYLE   "Auditory" has to do with listening and with speaking. *__Auditory learners__* **use their voices and their ears as the primary means of learning.** They recall what they hear and what they themselves express verbally.

"When something is hard to understand, they want to talk it through," write professors Adele Ducharme and Luck Watford of Valdosta State University in Georgia. "When they're excited and enthusiastic about learning, they want to verbally express their response. . . . These learners love class discussion, they grow by working and talking with others, and they appreciate a teacher taking time to explain something to them."[1]

Auditory learners may be easily distracted by sounds. Thus, if you're this type of person, it may be best that you not listen to the radio while studying, because you attend to all the sounds around you. An effective study technique, however, is to repeat something aloud several times because that will help you memorize it. These types of learners may do well learning foreign languages, music, and other areas that depend on a strong auditory sense.

VISUAL LEARNING STYLE   "Visual," of course, refers to the sense of sight. *__Visual learners__* **like to see pictures of things described or words written down.** "They will seek out illustrations, diagrams, and charts to help them understand and remember information," say Ducharme and Watford. "They appreciate being able to follow what a teacher is presenting with material written on an overhead transparency or in a handout."

If you are a visual learner, an effective technique for reviewing and studying material may be to read over your notes and recopy and reorganize information in outline form. Elsewhere we discuss mind maps, pyramids, and other ways of organizing information in a visual way.

KINESTHETIC LEARNING STYLE   "Kinesthetic" ("kin-es-*thet*-ik") has to do with the sense of touch and of physical manipulation. *__Kinesthetic learners__*

learn best when they touch and are physically involved in what they are studying. These are the kind of people who fidget when they have to sit still and who express enthusiasm by jumping up and down.

"These learners want to act out a situation, to make a product, to do a project, and in general to be busy with their learning," say Ducharme and Watford. "They find that when they physically do something, they understand it and they remember it."

If you are a kinesthetic learner, you may find you like courses in which you can become physically involved—physical education courses, certainly, but also some theater courses, art courses (such as sculpture), and science courses (laboratory courses in chemistry and biology).

MIXED-MODALITY LEARNING STYLE   "Modality" ("moh-*dal*-it-ee") means style. As you might guess, ***mixed-modality learners* are able to function in all three of these learning styles or "modalities"—auditory, visual, and kinesthetic.** Clearly, these people are at an advantage because they can handle information in whatever way it is presented to them.

Distance learning would seem to favor some kinds of learning styles over others. (There may not be much opportunity, for instance, to learn kinesthetically.) But just because you seem to favor one kind of learning, *it's very important that you not assume you are therefore limited or deficient in other areas*. People are not constrained by particular kinds of learning preferences. If you're less effective at one form of learning style than another, there are ways to bring about improvements, as we discuss later in this chapter.

THE STAGES OF LEARNING: HOW TO USE BLOOM'S TAXONOMY TO BE A SUCCESSFUL DL STUDENT

In the 1950s, Benjamin Bloom and his colleagues presented a so-called *taxonomy*— meaning hierarchy—of thinking skills that college work requires.[2] ***Bloom's taxonomy* describes a hierarchy of six critical-thinking skills: (1) two lower-order skills—*memorization* and *comprehension;* and (2) four higher-order skills—*application, analysis, synthesis*, and *evaluation*.** You may be able to get through some courses by simply memorizing facts and comprehending the basic ideas—that is, using the lower-order skills. But to really become engaged with the subject matter, you'll need to employ the four higher-order critical-thinking skills.

Let's consider how you can take advantage of this knowledge. By advancing through these stages as you study a topic, you'll be better able to retain the information and thus do better on exams.

MEMORIZE—"I CAN RECOGNIZE AND RECALL THE INFORMATION"   Could you study history without memorizing names and some dates? Could you study even archery, yoga, or free-hand drawing without having to recall certain facts? To think about a subject, you have to have facts to think about. The first of the lower-order critical-thinking skills, *memorization* consists of recognizing information in its original form and recalling information in its original form. Learning always begins with memorizing because you have to have a solid base of knowledge about the subject before you can proceed. Thus, your instructors will expect you to be able to recognize familiar terms, complete objective lists, and enumerate lists of key words.

Example: In studying how an organization works, you need to be able to describe its five principal departments or functions: Production, Research & Development, Accounting & Finance, Marketing, and Personnel.

COMPREHEND—"I CAN RECALL INFORMATION IN MY OWN TERMS AND EXPLAIN THEM TO A FRIEND"   You could memorize all the ingredients in a recipe, but if you don't comprehend how they are supposed to go together, could you cook them in an edible dish? The second of the lower-order critical-thinking skills, *comprehension* is the ability to recall information or concepts on your own terms. The best way to determine whether you've achieved comprehension is to be able to easily explain concepts to a friend who is not familiar with them.

Example: Explaining to a friend the five functions of an organization, you might say they all have to do with making or selling a product. "Research & Development thinks up the product, Production makes it, Marketing sells it, Accounting & Finance keeps track of costs and sales, and Personnel hires and fires the people who do the other four functions."

APPLY—"I CAN APPLY WHAT I'VE LEARNED TO A NEW AREA"   The first of the higher-order critical concepts, *application* consists of extending the information you've memorized and comprehended to new areas. Application is the start of problem solving.

Example: You might have already learned the five functions or departments of a for-profit organization, such as a computer maker. But you also see that you can apply these departments to a nonprofit organization, such as a hospital. The "product" being delivered is health care. Research & Development is medical and health research. Production is the care of patients. Marketing is advertisement of the hospital's services. Accounting & Finance is the billing office. Personnel is hiring of physicians, nurses, and so on.

ANALYZE—"I CAN BREAK APART THESE IDEAS AND RELATE THEM TO OTHER CONCEPTS"   *Analysis,* the second of the higher-order critical concepts, consists of identifying the parts of an idea and seeing how they are related. This is the critical skill you're executing when a professor asks you to "compare and contrast" on an essay exam. It's also a skill you'll use when you're identifying the assumptions or values underlying a concept.

Example: You could use the five functions to analyze Apple Computer back in the early 1980s, when founders Steve Jobs and Stephen Wozniak were inventing the personal computer in a Palo Alto, California, garage. You could analyze the company again after the company had fired Jobs and was doing poorly under new managers, and then a third time when Jobs was lured back and began originating some distinctive products, such as the iMac.

SYNTHESIZE—"I CAN BUILD ON OTHER KNOWLEDGE TO PUT TOGETHER THE ELEMENTS TO FORM A NEW WHOLE" The third of the thinking concepts, *synthesis* consists of putting together the elements, along with other knowledge you have, to produce a new perspective.

Example: What if you were to apply the five functions to constructing something a bit unusual—for example, a new college eating club?

EVALUATION—"I CAN USE ALL THESE THINKING SKILLS TO FORM A JUDGMENT" *Evaluation*, the final higher-order thinking skill, consists of making well-reasoned judgments.

Example: As a hypothetical venture capitalist, you might be required to evaluate unusual business plans that you're considering financing: an Amway-style organization to sell cemetery plots, an adoption program for wild horses found on government lands, an online distribution system for gardening services.

Now let's go back to the beginning of Bloom's taxonomy and see what you can do to improve your beginning learning skills—memorization and comprehension.

Memory & Forgetting: The Importance of Managing Long-Term Memory

How good is your memory? **_Memory_ is defined as a mental process that entails three main operations: recording, storage, and recall.** More plainly, "memory is the persistence of information," as one scholar calls it.[3]

The main strategy at work seems to be **_association_—one idea reminds you of another.**[4] Actually, even though you may worry that you have a weak memory because you immediately forget people's names after being introduced to them at a party, it's probably just fine. But how well are you using it in studying?

"I CRAM, THEREFORE I AM" Your mind holds a wonderful mishmash of names, addresses, telephone numbers, pictures, familiar routes, words to songs, and hundreds of thousands of other facts. How did you learn them—during several hours late one night or repeatedly over a long time? The answer is obvious.

When it comes to school, however, many students try to study for exams by doing a great deal of the work of a semester or quarter all in one night or in a couple of days. This is the time-dishonored memorizing marathon known as **_cramming_, defined as preparing hastily for an examination.**

Many students have the notion that facts can be remembered best if they're fresh. This notion is true—up to a point, as we'll discuss. But does cramming work? Certainly it beats the alternative of not studying at all.

Suppose, however, you crammed all night to memorize the lines for a character in a play. And suppose also that the next morning, instead of going to an examination room, you had to get up on a stage and recite the entire part. Could you do it? Probably not. Yet the quarter or semester's worth of material you have tried overnight to jam into your memory banks for a test may be even more comprehensive than all the lines an actor has to memorize for a play.

In sum: Even if you found cramming a successful exam-preparation technique in high school, we strongly recommend you begin now to find other techniques for memorizing. In higher education there is simply too much to learn.

THE FORGETTING CURVE: FAST-FADING MEMORIES   To understand why, from the standpoint of learning in higher education, long-term memory is so important, consider what psychologists call the "forgetting curve." In one famous experiment long ago, Hermann Ebbinghaus found that, in memorizing nonsense syllables, a great deal of information is forgotten just during the first 24 hours, then it levels out.[5] Although you (fortunately) need not memorize nonsense syllables, the rate of forgetting also occurs just as rapidly for prose (that is, ordinary language) and poetry. Interestingly, however, poetry is easier to memorize than prose because it has built-in memory cues such as rhymes, a trick you can use (as we'll show under "Improve Your Memory Power").

How good are people at remembering things in the normal course of events?

According to a survey from the National Institute for Development and Administration at the University of Texas, we remember only

10 percent of what we read,
20 percent of what we hear,
30 percent of what we see,
50 percent of what we see and hear,
70 percent of what we say, and
90 percent of what we do and say.[6]

One scholar, Walter Pauk, reports a study of people who read a textbook chapter in which it was found that they forgot

46 percent of what they read after 1 day,
79 percent of what they read after 14 days, and
81 percent of what they read after 28 days.[7]

As for remembering what one has heard, Pauk describes an experiment in which a group of psychologists who attended a seminar forgot over 91 percent of what they had heard after two weeks.[8]

If you were tested every other day on the study materials you heard and read, memorizing wouldn't be much of a problem. But that's not the way it usually works, of course. Ordinarily an instructor will give you an exam halfway or a third of the way into the course, perhaps another exam later, followed by a final exam at the end of the course. Each time you will be held accountable for several weeks' worth of lectures and readings. On the last exam, you're usually held responsible for the entire content of the course. Once again, we see that persistence—your ability to persevere—is important.

Memory is also important in writing papers. If you start your research or writing and then abandon it for a couple of weeks, it will take you extra time to reconnect with your thoughts when you go back to it.

HOW TO IMPROVE YOUR MEMORY POWER: CONCERTED MEMORIZATION

Success in school principally lies with a strategy in which you convert short-term memories into long-term memories. In this section we'll describe variations on the drill-and-practice type of learning.

PRACTICE REPEATEDLY—EVEN OVERLEARN MATERIAL   How well could you perform a part in a play or a movie after two readings? five readings? fifteen?

Clearly, you can't just speed-read or skim the script. You have to actively practice or rehearse the material. The more you rehearse, the better you retain information. Indeed, it has been found that overlearning—continued study even after you think you have learned material—will help you really commit it to memory.[9] ***Overlearning* is defined as continued rehearsal of material after you first appear to have mastered it**.[10] Overlearning is another way of saying "persistence."

A good way to learn is to repeatedly test your knowledge in order to rehearse it. Some textbooks come with self-testing study guides to help you do this, but you can also make up the questions yourself or form a study group with friends to trade questions and answers.

The more you rehearse, in fact, the better you may also understand the material.[11] This is because, as you review, your mind begins to concentrate on the most important features, thus helping your understanding.

The rule, then, is: Study or practice repeatedly to fix material firmly in mind. You can apply this rule to your social life, too. If you meet someone new at a party, for instance, you can repeat the person's name on being introduced, then say it again to yourself; then wait a minute and say it again.

STUDY A LITTLE AT A TIME FREQUENTLY: DISTRIBUTED PRACTICE VERSUS MASSED PRACTICE   Learning experts distinguish between two kinds of learning or practice techniques: massed practice and distributed practice.

- ***Massed practice:*** Massed practice is what students do when they are cramming. ***Massed practice* is putting all your studying into one long period of time**—for example, one 8-hour study session.
- ***Distributed practice:*** Distributed practice takes no more time than cramming. **With *distributed practice*, you spread the same number of hours over several days**—for example, four days of studying 2 hours a day.

Distributed practice has been found to be more effective for retaining information than mass practice, especially if the space between practice periods is reasonably long, such as 24 hours.[12] One reason is that studying something at different times links it to a wider variety of associations.[13]

The rule here, therefore, is to study or practice a little at a time frequently rather than a lot infrequently. If you're studying large amounts of factual material, try studying for 45 minutes, then take a break. Review the material, then take another break. You can also do this with small tasks of memorization. "Want to memorize the names of 10 bones? Study the list for several minutes," suggests one writer, "then go on to another task. Go back to the list, say it out loud, write it out. Review it. Then take another break and return to the list a third time, using whatever concentration techniques work best for you. Now test your recall. You'll find it much better than if you'd just studied for 25 minutes without a break."[14]

This rule also suggests you can make use of the time-spaces in your day for studying. You can look over your notes or books or flash cards while on the bus, for example, or waiting for class to start. You can mentally rehearse lists while standing in line at the grocery store or lunch counter. It's like the difference between lifting weights for one 5-hour session or five sessions of 1 hour each: The first way won't train you nearly as well as the second way.

AVOID INTERFERENCE   Learning some kinds of information will interfere with your ability to recall other kinds of information, especially if the subjects are similar. ***Interference* is the competition among related memories**. For example, if you tried to memorize the names of the bones in the human foot and then memorize the names of the bones in the hand, one memory might interfere with the other. And the more information you learn, such as lists of words, the more you may have trouble with new information on successive days, such as new lists of words.[15]

Interference can also come from other things, such as distractions from background music, television, the people with whom you share your living space, and so on. The notion of interference also suggests why you do better at recalling information when it is fresh in your mind. In other words, though we don't recommend cramming for exams, we do recommend giving information a thorough last-minute review before you go into the test. A last-minute review puts the "frosting on the cake" of helping you absorb the material, but it's no substitute for studying the material earlier.

The lesson here is this: When you're trying to memorize material, don't study anything else that is too similar too soon. This is why it is often a good idea to study before going to sleep: The chances of the new information getting competition from other information is reduced.[16] It also shows why it's a good idea to study similar material for different courses on different days.[17]

HOW TO IMPROVE YOUR MEMORY POWER

Does practice make perfect? Probably it does for some things, as in repeatedly making basketball free throws. However, as Bloom's taxonomy points out, the best way is to use your comprehension, analysis, synthesis, and other higher-order learning skills. In line with these ideas, you might try the following techniques:

MAKE MATERIAL MEANINGFUL TO YOU: DEPTH OF PROCESSING
Information in memory may be stored at a superficial level or at a deep level, depending on how well you understood it and how much you thought about it, according to the ***depth-of-processing principle***.[18] **This states that how shallowly or deeply you hold a thought depends on how much you think about it and how many associations you form with it.** The deeper the level of "processing," or thinking, the better you remember it.

This means that, to memorize something, you shouldn't just mindlessly repeat the material; you are better able to remember it when you can make it meaningful.[19] It's important to somehow make the material your own—understand it, organize it, put it in your own words, develop emotional associations toward it, link it with information you already know or events you have already experienced. For example, if you are trying to remember that business organizations have departments that perform five functions—accounting, marketing, production, personnel management, and research—you can look for relationships among them. Which departments do or do not apply to you? Which ones do your relatives work in? Indeed, one way to make material meaningful to you is to organize it in some way, which is why outlining your reading can be a useful tool.

To repeat, *the rule here is to make learning personally meaningful to you.*

USE VERBAL MEMORY AIDS   One way to make information more meaningful, and so retain it better, is to use memory aids—and the more you are able to personalize them, the more successful they will be. Psychologists call such memory aids ***mnemonic*** ("nee-*mahn*-ik") ***devices***, **tactics for making things memorable by making them distinctive.** The devices that work best for you relate to your learning style. For example, verbal memory aids work best for auditory learners.

Some verbal devices for enhancing memory are as follows:

- ***Write out your information.*** This advice may seem obvious. Still, the evidence is that if you write out a shopping list, for example, then if you lose the list, you are more apt to remember the items than if you didn't write them out.

  Clearly, this is a reason to take notes during a lecture, quite apart from making a record: The very act of writing helps you retain information. Even better, if you don't simply write mindlessly but attempt to inject the material with personal meaning, you'll remember it even better.

- ***Organize your information.*** People are better able to memorize material when they can organize it. This is one reason why imposing a ranking or hierarchy, such as an outline, on lecture notes or reading notes works so well, especially when the material is difficult.[20]

  Thus, to learn lists, try grouping items that have similar meanings. "If you need to remember Queen Victoria, Charlotte Brontë, Prince Albert, and Charles Dickens," suggests one writer, "mentally split the group into males and females, or writers and royals."[21]

- *Use rhymes to remember important ideas.* You may have heard the spelling rule "I before E except after C" (so that you'll spell "receive," not "recieve"). This an example of the use of rhyme as a memory aid. Another is "Thirty days hath September, April, June, and November . . . " to remember which months have 30 rather than 31 days.

  Most of the time, of course, you'll have to make up your own rhymes. It doesn't matter that they are silly. Indeed, the sillier they are, the more apt you may be to remember them.

- *Use phrases whose first letters represent ideas you want to remember.* Probably the first thing music students learn is "**E**very **G**ood **B**oy **D**oes **F**ine" to remember what notes designate the lines of the musical staff: E G B D F. This is an *acrostic*—a phrase in which the first letter of each word is a cue to help you recall words or concepts beginning with the same letter.

  What kind of sentence would you make up to remember that business organizations have departments performing five functions—Accounting, Marketing, Production, Personnel management, and Research? (Maybe it would be, "**A**ny **M**an **P**laying **P**oker is **R**ich"—this also plants a picture in your mind that will help your recall.)

- *Use a word whose first letters represent ideas you want to remember.* To remember the five business functions above, you could switch the words around and have the nonsense word PRAMP (to rhyme with "ramp," then think of, say, a wheelchair ramp or a ramp with a pea rolling down it), the letters of which stand for the first letters of the five functions. (This is an *acronym*.)

  A common example of the use of this device is the name *Roy G. Biv*, which students use to memorize the order of colors in the light spectrum: **r**ed, **o**range, **y**ellow, **g**reen, **b**lue, **i**ndigo, **v**iolet. HOMES is the acronym used to memorize the names of the Great Lakes: **H**uron, **O**ntario, **M**ichigan, **E**rie, **S**uperior.

- *Make up a narrative story that associates words.* A technique known as the **_narrative story method_** **helps students recall unrelated lists of words by giving them meaning and linking them in a specific order.**[22]

  Suppose you need to memorize the words *rustler, penthouse, mountain, sloth, tavern, fuzz, gland, antler, pencil, vitamin*. This is quite a mixed bag, but if you were taking a French class, you might have to memorize these words (in that language). Here is the story that was constructed to help recall these unrelated words:

  "A Rustler lived in a Penthouse on top of a Mountain. His specialty was the three-toed Sloth. He would take his captive animals to a Tavern, where he would remove Fuzz from their Glands. Unfortunately, all this exposure to sloth fuzz caused him to grow Antlers. So he gave up his profession and went to work in a Pencil factory. As a precaution he also took a lot of Vitamin E."[23]

  In using verbal memory tricks, then, *the rule is to make up verbal cues that are meaningful to you to represent or associate ideas.* In social situations, as when you are introduced to several people simultaneously, you can try using some of these devices. For example, "LAP" might represent Larry, Ann, and Paul.

USE VISUAL MEMORY AIDS   Some psychologists think that using visual images creates a second set of cues in addition to verbal cues that can help memorization.[24] In other words, it helps if you can mentally "take photographs" of the material you are trying to retain.

There are two visual memory aids you may find useful—a single unusual visual image, or a series of visual images.

- *Make up a vivid, unusual picture to associate ideas.* The stranger and more distinctive you can make your image, the more you are apt to be able to remember it.

  Thus, to remember the five business functions (Research, Accounting, Marketing, Personnel management, Production), you might create a picture of a woman with a white laboratory coat (Research) looking through a magnifying glass at a man who is a'counting money (Accounting) while sitting in a food-market shopping cart (Marketing) that is being pushed by someone wearing a letter sweater that says *Person L* (Personnel) who is watching a lavish Hollywood spectacle—a production—on a movie screen (Production). (If you wish, you could even draw a little sketch of this while you're trying to memorize it.)

- *Make up a story of vivid images to associate ideas.* A visual trick called the ___method of loci___ ("*loh*-sigh," meaning "places") **is to memorize a series of places and then use a different vivid image to associate each place with an idea or a word you want to remember**.

  For example, you might use buildings and objects along the route from your house to your campus or workplace, or from the parking lot to a classroom or office, and associate each one with a specific word or idea. Again, the image associated with each location should be as distinctive as you can make it. To remember the information, you imagine yourself proceeding along this route, so that the various locations cue the various ideas. (The locations need not resemble the ideas. For example, you might associate a particular tree with a man in a white laboratory coat in its branches—Research.)

In short, when using visual memory tricks, *the rule is this: The stranger you make the picture, the more you are apt to remember it.*

THE FIVE-STEP SQ3R READING SYSTEM

"There's a war on! We must teach them to read faster!"

Maybe that's what psychologist Francis P. Robinson was told in 1941. In any event, Robinson then set about to devise an intensified reading system for World War II military people enrolled in special courses at Ohio State University. Since then, many thousands of students have successfully used his system or some variation to learn to read more effectively.

The reason the system is effective is that it breaks a reading assignment down into manageable portions that require you to understand them before you move on.

Robinson's reading system, called the ***SQ3R reading method,*** **consists of five steps: Survey, Question, Read, Recite, Review.**[25] Let's see how you would apply these to the chapter of a textbook you are assigned to read.

STEP 1: S—SURVEY   A survey is an overview: You do a quick 1- or 2-minute overview of the entire chapter before you plunge into it. Look at the advance organizers—the chapter outline or learning objectives, if any; the chapter headings; and the summary, if any, at the end of the chapter. The point of surveying is twofold:

- ***You establish relationships among the major segments.*** Surveying enables you to see how the chapter segments go together. Understanding how the parts fit in with the whole helps you see how the chapter makes sense.
- ***You see where you're going.*** If you know where you're going, you can better organize the information as you read. This is just like reading over directions to someone's house before you set out rather than bit by bit while traveling.

Next you apply Steps 2 through 4—Question, Read, Recite—but only to one section at a time, or to an even smaller segment. That is, you apply the next three steps section by section (or even paragraph by paragraph if material is difficult). You apply Step 5, Review, only after you have finished the chapter.

STEP 2: Q—QUESTION   Take a look at the heading of the first section and turn it into a question in your mind. For example, if the heading (in a book about computers) is "Basic Software Tools for Work and Study," ask "What does 'Basic Software Tools' mean?" If the heading is to a subsection, do the same. For example, if the heading is "Word Processing," ask, "How does word processing work?"

Questioning has two important effects:

- ***You become personally involved.*** By questioning, you get actively involved in your reading. And personal involvement is one of the most fundamental ways to commit information to memory.
- ***You identify the main ideas.*** Giving the heading this kind of attention pinpoints the principal ideas you are now going to read about. And it is the main ideas that are important, after all, not the supporting details.

    If you are proceeding on a paragraph-by-paragraph basis because the material is difficult (as in technical courses such as physics), there may not be any heading that you can convert to a question. In that case, you'll need to put Step 3, Read, before Step 2: That is, you read the paragraph, then create a question about that paragraph.

Incidentally, it's perfectly all right (indeed, even desirable) at this stage to move your lips and ask the question under your breath.

STEP 3: R—READ   Now you actually do the reading—but only up to the next section heading (or paragraph). Note, however, that you do not read as though you were reading a popular novel. Rather, you read *with purpose*—actively searching to answer the question you posed. If you don't seem to understand it, reread the section until you can answer the question.

What is the difference between passive and active reading? If you were reading a murder mystery *passively*, you would just run your eyes over the lines and wait, perhaps mildly curious, to see how things came out. If you were reading that mystery novel *actively*, you would constantly be trying to guess the outcome. You would be asking yourself such questions as: Who is the killer? What was that strange phone call about? What motive would she have for the murder? What was that funny business in his background? And you would be searching for the answers while you read.

You don't need to do that with recreational reading. Reading a textbook or work-related document, however, should *always* be an active process of asking questions and searching for answers. That's why you have to take study breaks from time to time (perhaps 5 minutes every half hour, or even every 15 minutes, if the material is difficult), because this type of reading is not effortless.

In addition, especially if the segment is somewhat long, you should read (perhaps on a second reading) for another purpose:

- ***Determine whether the section asks any other questions.*** The question you formulated based on the section heading may not cover all the material in the segment. Thus, as you read, you may see other questions that should be asked about the material.
- ***Ask those questions and answer them.*** You probably get the idea: The Question and Read steps are not completely separate steps. Rather, you are continually alternating questions and answers as you read through the segment.

    Some examples of questions you might frame in your mind as you read a textbook are these:

    What is the main idea of this paragraph?
    What is an example that illustrates this principle?
    What are the supporting facts?
    Who is this person and why is he or she considered important?
    What could the instructor ask me about this on the exam?
    What about this don't I understand?

If necessary, as you identify and think about key points, you may want to write brief notes to trigger your memory when you get to Step 5, Review.

STEP 4: R—RECITE   When you reach the end of the section, stop and look away from the page. *Recite* the answer you have just discovered for the question you formulated. You should practice this in two ways:

- ***Recite the answer aloud.*** We don't mean so loud that you have other riders on the bus looking at you. But there's nothing embarrassing about talking *subvocally* to yourself—that is, moving your tongue within your mouth while your lips move imperceptibly. Moving the muscles in your lips and mouth and throat helps lay down a memory trace in your mind.

We can't stress enough the importance of reciting aloud or nearly aloud. As Walter Pauk writes, "Reciting promotes concentration, forms a sound basis for understanding the next paragraph or the next chapter, provides time for the memory trace to consolidate, ensures that facts and ideas are remembered accurately, and provides immediate feedback on how you're doing."[26] Pauk also mentions experiments that show that students who read and recite learn much better than students who just read.

- *Say the answer in your own words.* When you formulate the answer in your own words (perhaps using an example) rather than just repeat a phrase off the page, you are required to *understand* it rather than just memorize it. And when you understand it, you *do* memorize it better.

    If you did not take any notes for review earlier, you may wish to at this point. The notes should not be extensive, just brief cues to jog your memory when you move to Step 5, Review.

Don't move on to the next segment until you're sure you understand this one. After all, if you don't get it now, when will you? Once you think you understand the section, move on to the next section (or paragraph) and repeat steps 2, 3, and 4.

STEP 5: R—REVIEW   When you have read all the way through the chapter (or as far as you intend to go in one study session) section by section in Question-Read-Recite fashion, you are ready to test how well you have mastered your key ideas. Here's how to do it:

- *Go back over the book's headings or your notes and ask the questions again.* Repeat the questions and try to answer them without looking at the book or your notes. If you have difficulty, check your answers.
- *Review other memory aids.* Read the chapter summary and the review questions. Then skim the chapter again, as well as your notes, refreshing your memory.

LECTURES & CLASS MEETINGS

If you do not have the chalk-and-talk sort of lecture that you've been accustomed to in school, you may want to skip this discussion. With live broadcast telecourses or with prerecorded videos, however, it's important to get comfortable with the lecture method of teaching. Here you have two tasks:

- *Be able to extract material.* You need to be able to extract the most information out of a lecture—that is, take useful notes, regardless of your learning preference and the instructor's style.
- *Be able to learn material.* You need to be able to learn the lecture material so that you can do well on tests.

BEING AN ACTIVE PARTICIPANT: PREPARING FOR CLASS   How do you approach the whole matter of being involved in a course? In a traditional class, do you sit in the back, find yourself constantly distracted during lectures, have difficulty taking notes? Being a distance learner means taking an active, involved approach to the course. Try to prepare for your upcoming classes or online meetings by doing the following:

- ***Use the syllabus as a basic "roadmap" to the course.*** As discussed in Chapter 1 (page 9) **the _syllabus_ is a course outline or guide that tells you what readings are required, what assignments are due when, and when examinations are scheduled.**

  It's a good idea to three-hole punch the syllabus and include it in the front of your binder or staple it inside the front of your notebook. That way you will automatically have it available and can make any changes to it that the instructor announces (such as a new date for a test). Active learners are always anticipating the requirements of the course.
- ***Do the homework before the class meeting.*** A syllabus will often show that certain readings coincide with certain class meetings or lectures. It usually works best if you do the readings *before* rather than after. Like putting your toe in the water, this will help you know what to expect. If you do the homework first, you'll understand the instructor's remarks better.

LEARNING TO FOCUS YOUR ATTENTION   Once you're in a class meeting, what do you do then? You learn to pay attention. Being attentive involves active listening and active observing, which is different from the kind of passive attention used to watch and listen to television. Active listening is, in one writer's description, "paying attention so that your brain absorbs the meaning of words and sentences."[27]

One way to do this is to observe so-called bell phrases and bell cues that your instructor gives in any presentation, phrases and gestures that "ring a bell" and signal importance.

- ***Bell phrase:* A _bell phrase_—also called a "signal word" or "signal phrase"—is an indicator of an important point.** Bell phrases signal that you should note and remember what comes after them. Examples of bell phrases are: "Three major types . . ."; "The most important result is . . ."; "You should remember . . ."; "Because of this . . ."; "First . . . second . . . third . . ."
- ***Bell cue:* A _bell cue_ is an instructor's action or gesture that indicates important points.** Examples are (1) diagrams or charts; (2) notes on the whiteboard; (3) pointing, as to something on the board or a chart; (4) underlining of or making a check mark by key words; (5) banging a fist; and (6) holding up fingers.

When a class is long or tedious, you can turn it into a game by telling yourself you will try to detect as many bell phrases and cues as possible. Then, every time you pick one up, put a check mark in your notes. When you do this, you'll find yourself becoming more actively involved. Not only does it fight boredom and fatigue, but it also increases the quality of your note taking.

LEARNING TO OVERCOME COURSE OBSTACLES   What do you do if, for example, you're videoconferencing and the instructor speaks too fast or with an accent? If your shorthand or ear is not good enough to keep up, try these strategies:

- ***Do your homework before the meeting.*** If you keep up with the reading assignments, doing them before the class meeting rather than afterward, you'll often be able to mentally fill in gaps, recognize unfamiliar phrases, and identify key points.
- ***Leave holes in your notes.*** Whenever you miss something important, leave spaces in your notes, with a big question mark in the margin. Then seek to fill in the missing material through other methods, as explained below.
- ***Trade notes with classmates.*** If you and others in class take readable notes (even using private shorthand), you can easily make photocopies of your notes and exchange them. Two or three students may find that among them they are able to pick up most of an instructor's remarks.
- ***Use a tape recorder.*** The trick here is *not* to make a tape recorder a substitute for note taking. Then you'll merely be taking the same amount of time to listen to the lecture again—and perhaps still be confused. Use the tape recorder as a backup system, in which you can use the fast-forward and reverse buttons to go over material you had trouble following in class.
- ***Ask questions.*** If the instructor has a question period, such as a chat room or threaded discussion time, you can ask questions to clarify what you missed. Or contact the instructor via e-mail.

THE 5R STEPS: RECORD, REWRITE, RECITE, REFLECT, REVIEW

Many students have the idea that they can simply take notes at a class meeting or lecture and then review them whenever it's convenient—perhaps the night before a test. And it's easy to think you are doing well when you attend every class and fill page after page of your notebook.

However, simply writing everything down—acting like a human tape recorder—by itself doesn't work. *The name of the game, after all, is to learn the material, not just make a record of it.* Writing things down now but saving all the learning for later is simply not efficient. As we discussed, research shows that most forgetting takes place within the first 24 hours, then drops off. The trick, then, is to figure out how to reduce the forgetting of that first 24 hours.

Effective learning requires that you be not only a good note *taker* but also a good note *reviewer*. This may mean you need to change the note-taking and note-learning approach you're accustomed to. However, once these new skills are learned, you'll find them invaluable.

One helpful method is known as the **5R steps, for Record, Rewrite, Recite, Reflect, Review.** They are

- ***Step 1—Record:*** Capture the main ideas.
- ***Step 2—Rewrite:*** Following the class meeting, rewrite your notes, developing key terms, questions, and summaries.
- ***Step 3—Recite:*** Cover up the key terms, questions, and summaries and practice reciting them to yourself.

- ***Step 4—Reflect:*** To anchor these ideas, make some personal association with them.
- ***Step 5—Review:*** Two or three times a week, if possible, review your notes to make them more familiar.

Studies show that increased practice or rehearsal not only increases retention, it also improves your *understanding* of material, because as you go over it repeatedly, you are able to concentrate on the most important points. This is in line with the Bloom's taxonomy, which involves both memorization and comprehension. You probably can appreciate this from your own experience in having developed some athletic, musical, or other skill: The more you did it, the better you got. Like an actor, the more you practice or rehearse the material, the better you will be able to overcome stage fright and deliver your best performance on examination day.

Let's consider the five steps:

STEP 1: RECORD   In a traditional course, you'll see many of your classmates with pens racing to try to capture every word of the lecture. Don't bother. You're not supposed to be like a court reporter or a secretary-stenographer, recording every word. You should be less concerned with taking down everything than in developing a system of note taking. Here is how the system works.

- ***Leave blank margins on your note page.*** This is a variation on what is known as the *Cornell format* of note taking. Draw a vertical line, top to bottom, 1½ inches from the left edge of the paper, a similar line 1½ inches from the right side, and a horizontal line 1½ inches up from the bottom. As we explain, you will use these blank margins for review purposes.
- ***Take notes in rough paragraph form.*** At some point you may have been told to take notes in outline form, using the standard "I, A, 1, a," format. If you're good at this, that's fine. However, most professors don't lecture this way, and you should not have to concentrate on trying to force an outline on their material.

  Simply take your notes in rough paragraph form. Put extra space (a line or two) between new ideas and divisions of thought. Don't try to save on the cost of notepaper by cramming notes onto every line of the page.
- ***Try to capture the main ideas.*** Don't try to take down everything the instructor says. Not only will this create a mass of information that you will have to sort through later, it will also interfere with your learning. Instead of forcing you to pay attention and concentrate on what's important, you become simply a mindless tape recorder. You want to be a *mindful* note taker. An extremely important part of your note-taking system, then, is to try to capture just the key ideas.
- ***Develop a system of abbreviations.*** Some people take highly readable notes, as though preparing to let other people borrow them. You shouldn't concern yourself primarily with this kind of legibility. The main thing is that you be able to take ideas down fast so that *you* can read them later.

  Thus, make up your own system of abbreviations. For example, "w.r.t" means "with regard to"; "sike" means "psychology"; "para" is borrowing the Spanish word for "in order to."

By adopting these practices, you'll be well on your way to retaining more information than you have in the past.

STEP 2: REWRITE   The point of this *extremely important* step is to counteract the brain's natural tendency to forget 80 percent of the information in the first 24 hours.

As soon as possible—on the same day in which you took lecture notes—you should do one of two things:

1. *Either recopy/rewrite your notes, or*
2. *At least go over them to familiarize yourself with and underline key issues and concepts and to make notations in the margins.*

This activity will give you the extra familiarization that will help to imprint the information in your mind. If you use the word processing program on your computer, the rewriting is not as time consuming as it sounds.

By rewriting and underlining you reinforce the material, moving it from short-term into long-term memory. Here's what to do:

- **Read, rewrite, and highlight your notes.** Read your notes over. If you can, rewrite them—copy them over in a separate notebook or type them up on a word processor—with the same margins at the left, right, and bottom as described above. Now read the notes again, using highlighter pen or underlining to emphasize key ideas.
- **Write key terms in the left margin.** In the left margins, write the key terms and main concepts. Reviewing these important terms and concepts is a good way to prepare for objective questions, such as true/false or multiple-choice, on tests.
- **Write one or two questions in the right margin.** On the right side of each page, write two questions about the material on the page. Reviewing these questions later will help you prepare for tests featuring essay questions or subjective questions.
- **Write a summary on the last page.** At the bottom of the last page of that day's notes, summarize in a few words the material in the notes. Some students write these summaries in red or green ink. With this eye-catching color, they can then flip through their notes and quickly take in all the summary information.

If you don't have time or aren't strongly motivated to rewrite your notes, do at least take 5 or 10 minutes to fill in the blank margins you left around your notes.

We cannot stress enough how important it is to take time—absolutely no later than one day after your class—to go over your notes, rewriting them if you can but certainly writing key terms, questions, and summaries at the end.

STEP 3: RECITE   Another reinforcement technique is *recitation*. This consists of covering up your detailed notes and using the key terms or concepts in the left margin to say out loud (or under your breath to yourself) what you understand your notes to mean. You can also do this with the questions in the right margin and the summary in the bottom margin.

Recitation is an activity you can do at your desk when you're doing homework or when you have 5 or 10 minutes of free time during the day. It is a particularly effective reinforcing technique because the activity of verbalizing gives your mind time to grasp the ideas and move them from short-term to long-term memory.

STEP 4: REFLECT   Reflecting is also something you can do in small bits of free time throughout the day. Look over your notes from the previous class meeting in the course and try to make some *personal associations* in your mind with the material. Such personal associations will help to anchor the material. For example, if you're learning about European history, imagine how you might link some of these facts to a tour of Europe or to a movie you've seen that was set in that period.

STEP 5: REVIEW   Two or three times a week, review all your notes, using the techniques of recitation and reflection to commit the information to memory. At first you may find that the review takes longer, but as you get more familiar with the material the review will get easier. At the end of the semester or quarter you will then have perhaps 80 percent of the lecture or other information stored in your long-term memory. The remaining 20 percent can be learned in the days before the exam. Unlike the process of cramming, having this much material already memorized will give you much more confidence about your ability to succeed on the test.

TAKING CHARGE OF TAKING TESTS

As we discussed in Chapter 1, some distance learning instructors rely on other forms of student work besides testing (such as class projects) to gauge a student's progress and ability in the course. However, some distance learning students do take tests, often being asked to go to a certain location (such as a classroom on campus) where they take exams under the watchful eye of the instructor or a proctor.

Taking charge of taking tests has four components:

1. Psyching out the instructor
2. Learning how to prepare for specific tests
3. Knowing what to bring to the test
4. Getting started right in the testing room

Let's consider these.

PSYCHING OUT THE INSTRUCTOR   Instructors not only have different ways of teaching, but also different ways of testing. Some test mainly on the textbook, some mainly on the lecture material, some on both. It's up to you to be a detective—to figure out the instructor's method of operating and plan accordingly. This is usually not hard to do. The aim of an instructor, after all, is not to trick you but to find out what you know.

Following are some ways to get a jump on the test by finding out what the instructor will do:

- *Look at the course syllabus.* The syllabus (discussed on page 9) is often a good guide for test preparation. This basic road map to the course may tell you a lot about testing: It may tell you what kind of weight testing has in the overall course grade; whether (and how) low grades can be made up; or what happens if the test is missed. It may indicate if the lowest grade on a series of tests is dropped when the instructor is determining your average grade for all tests.
- *Look at instructor handouts.* Instructors may hand out potential essay questions in advance or prepare study guides. Handouts show what the instructor thinks is important. Like an actor learning your lines, you can use such material to practice taking the test. This can not only help prepare you by giving you sample material, it may also help reduce the stage fright–like condition known as "test anxiety."
- *Ask about the specific test.* Particularly before the first test in a class, when you don't know what's coming, make a point to ask the instructor the following:

  1. *How long will the test last?*
  2. *How much will the test results count toward the course grade?*
  3. *What types of questions will appear on the test? Will they be true/false? multiple-choice? fill-in? essay? all of these?* (Different questions require different test-taking strategies, as we'll explain under "The Six Step Examination Approach.")

  It's also fair to ask the instructor what is most important for you to know. Some instructors may emphasize certain subject areas over others, or they may emphasize the class-meeting or lecture material over the textbook.
- *Ask to see copies of old tests.* Some instructors may be willing to provide you with copies of old tests or with the kinds of questions they are inclined to ask. Don't feel it's somehow impolite or incorrect to ask to see old tests.
- *Consult students who have taken the course.* If you know others who have already taken the course, ask them about their test experiences. See if you can get them to share old exams so you can look at the kinds of questions the instructor likes to ask. Indeed, an item from an old test may even reappear on the one you will take, given that there are only so many ways to ask a question (but don't count on it).
- *In class meetings or lectures, listen for the instructor's bell phrases and bell cues.* As discussed above (p. 75), instructors often use phrases and gestures that should "ring a bell" and signal importance. Be sure to review your notes for these.

LEARNING TO PREPARE FOR A SPECIFIC TEST Following are strategies to employ when preparing for a specific test.

- *Rehearse study-guide or other practice questions.* Some textbook publishers produce a separate study guide, which you can buy at the campus bookstore. **A _study guide_ is a booklet that contains practice questions, along with their answers, covering material in the textbook.** For a fairly modest price, the study guide represents an excellent investment because it gives you a trial run at types of questions similar to those apt to be asked on the test.

A variation on the printed study guide now being seen more frequently is the ***electronic study guide*, which is a floppy disk that students can use on their personal computer to rehearse practice questions and check their answers.**

Some textbooks also have practice questions at the end of chapters, with answers to some or all of them in the back of the book.

- ***Form study groups with other students to generate practice questions.*** Forming study groups with some of your classmates is an excellent way to generate possible test questions—especially essay questions—and quiz one another on answers. Moreover, study groups offer reinforcement and inject a bit of social life into your studying. Study groups may be face-to-face, online, or on the telephone.

- ***Develop self-study practice sessions.*** Besides study guides and study groups, a useful preparation strategy is simply to have your own periodic practice sessions. Every week set aside time to go through your notes and textbooks and compose practice tests. Specifically:

  1. Practice reviewing material that is emphasized. This includes anything your instructor deems significant. Practice defining key terms, the terms presented in *italics* or **boldface** in the text. You can make excellent use of flash cards in this area. **A *flash card*, you may recall, is a card bearing words, numbers, or pictures that is briefly displayed as a learning aid.**

  2. Practice reviewing material that appears in numbered lists (such as the 13 vitamins or warning signs for heart disease). Enumerations often provide the basis for essay and multiple-choice questions.

  3. Practice answering questions on material about which you have a good many pages of coverage, either in text or lecture notes. Answer questions you've written in the text margins and in your lecture notes. Formulate essay questions and outline answers.

  4. When preparing, follow the Bloom's taxonomy approach described on pages 63–65.

     Memorization (the first lower-order critical-thinking skill) will be tested by these kinds of questions: true/false, multiple-choice, and fill-in-the-blank. These require you to identify terms and concepts.

     Comprehension (the second skill) will be tested by sentence-completion questions. Such questions require you to recall information or concepts on your own terms—as though you were to explain them to a friend.

     The higher-order skills—application, analysis, synthesis, and evaluation—will be tested by essay questions.

     Thus, when you're thinking up practice questions, try to cover all levels of critical-thinking skills.

- ***Study throughout the course.*** The best way to prepare for exams is not to play catch-up. Recall the idea of overlearning (discussed on page 67):

continuing to repeatedly review material even after you appear to have absorbed it. Of course, to overlearn you must first have learned. This means keeping up with lecture notes and textbooks, rereading them so that you really get to know the material. Space your studying rather than cramming, because it is repetition that will move information into your long-term memory bank.

- **Review the evening and morning before the test.** The night before a test, spend the evening reviewing your notes. Then go to bed without interfering (for instance, by watching television) with the material you have absorbed. Get plenty of rest—you won't need to stay up cramming if you've followed the suggestions in this book. The next morning, get up early and review your notes again.

THE SIX-STEP EXAMINATION APPROACH

The six-step system has three purposes: First, it is a very efficient method for tackling a test. Second, it helps you stave off panic because it gives you a plan to follow. Third, it helps you build confidence. The six steps are these:

1. Unload on the back of the test.
2. Review, but don't answer, the subjective questions.
3. Answer the objective questions.
4. Answer the subjective questions.
5. Answer questions left undone.
6. Proofread the examination.

STEP 1: UNLOAD ON THE BACK OF THE TEST   The first thing you should do after getting the test from your instructor is to put your name on it. (You'd be surprised how many students simply forget to sign their exam, baffling the instructor and delaying posting of the final grade.)

After signing it, *without looking at any of the questions,* flip the examination sheet over and simply *unload.* __Unloading__ **means taking 2–3 minutes to jot down on the back of the exam sheet any key words, concepts, and ideas that are in your mind.** These are things that you think might be on the test, and things you feel a bit shaky about—that is, things you've only recently studied and need to get down on paper while you still have them in mind.

Unloading is important for two reasons:

- **It relieves anxiety.** Just "blowing out" all the information pent up in your mind at the outset of the test can be extremely useful in helping overcome test anxiety.
- **It helps prevent forgetting.** One term or one idea can be like a string attached to a whole train of ideas that make up an entire essay. Unloading may well produce a key term or idea that leads to a mental string that you can pull on later in the test.

Unloading is neither illegal nor unethical. It is not cheating so long as the things you unload are the output of your own brain and not cribbed from elsewhere. (Ask for a blank piece of paper if you're not allowed to unload on the exam sheet.)

STEP 2: REVIEW, BUT DON'T ANSWER, THE SUBJECTIVE QUES-TIONS   After unloading, flip the test over. Skip over any objective questions (true/false, multiple-choice) and go to the ***subjective questions*—those that generally require long answers, such as essay-type questions, or those requiring lists as answers**. Examples are:

> *Compare and contrast the main schools of psychology.*
> *Describe the principal methods of textile making.*
> *List the four operations of a computer system.*

You should now take 2–3 minutes to do another form of unloading: Write key words in the margins next to each question. These key words will help to serve as a rough outline when you start answering. Don't, however, immediately begin writing answers to the subjective questions (unless these are the only kinds of questions on the exam). Rather, proceed to Step 3.

STEP 3: ANSWER THE OBJECTIVE QUESTIONS   *Objective questions* are the true/false, multiple-choice, matching, and fill-in questions. There's a good reason for answering objective questions first: *The very process of answering may supply details that will help you answer the subjective questions.* It may also help you answer a subjective question you didn't know when you reviewed it in Step 2.

This method uses the test as a tool. That is, your recognition of the answer to an objective question may help you to recall other material that may help you later in the test.

Answer the objective questions as quickly as you can. Don't spend any time on questions you're not sure of. Rather, circle or star them and return to them later.

STEP 4: ANSWER THE SUBJECTIVE QUESTIONS   When grading the test, instructors often assign more importance to some subjective questions than to others. That is, the answer to one question will be, say, 30 percent of the test grade and another will be 10 percent. Quite often the point values are shown on the examination sheet. If not, raise your hand and ask. It's your right as a student to know.

To make efficient use of your time, do the following:

- ***Read the directions!*** This obvious advice applies to all types of test questions. However, because subjective questions usually have higher point values, be sure you don't misunderstand the directions.
- ***EITHER answer the easiest first . . .*** Answer the easiest subjective questions first.
- ***. . . OR answer the highest-value questions first.*** Alternatively, answer the subjective questions with the greatest point values first.

STEP 5: ANSWER QUESTIONS LEFT UNDONE   By this point you will have answered the easiest questions or the ones that you have most knowledge about. As you get toward the end of the test period, now is your chance to go back and try answering the questions you left undone—those you circled or starred.

A word about guessing: *Unless the instructor or test says there's a penalty for guessing,* you might as well take a guess. (See the discussion under "Mastering Objective Questions" below.)

STEP 6: PROOFREAD THE EXAMINATION If you get through all your questions before the end of the examination period, it's tempting to hand in your test and walk out early. For one thing, you'll be dying to find relief from the pressure cooker. Secondly, you may think it somehow looks as if you're smarter if you're one of the first to leave. (However, it's not so. Often it's the ones who don't know the answers and have given up who leave early.)

The best strategy is, *if you have any time left, use it.* By staying, you give yourself The Extra Edge that the early leavers miss. During this remaining time, look over the test and *proofread* it. Correct any misspellings. Reread any questions to make sure you have fully understood them and responded to them correctly; make any changes necessary to your answers.

MASTERING OBJECTIVE QUESTIONS

As mentioned, objective questions are true/false, multiple-choice, matching, or fill-in-the blank questions. Objective questions can often be machine-scored. Such questions are called "objective" because the person doing the grading does not interpret or make judgment calls. By contrast, with "subjective," essay-type questions, the grader has some leeway in how to judge the worth of the answer.

Here are three general strategies to apply to objective questions:[28]

- *Guess, unless there's a penalty.* With objective questions, never leave an answer blank, *unless* the instructor or test says there's a penalty for guessing. Some instructors have grading systems for objective tests that penalize guessing (for example, a correct answer that counts +1, a nonresponse –1, and a wrong answer –2). Thus, be sure you know the ground rules before you guess.
- *If there are penalties for guessing, guess anyway if you can eliminate half the choices.* If the instructor does take points off for guessing, take a guess anyway when you can eliminate half or more of the options—for example, two out of four choices on a multiple-choice test.
- *Allow second thoughts, if you've prepared.* Answer objective questions reasonably quickly and put a star (★) next to any answer that you're unsure about. You may decide to change the answer when you do a final survey, based on information suggested to you by other items on the test.

  "Contrary to the popular advice about never changing answers, *it can be to your advantage to change answers,*" say educators Tim Walter and Al Siebert (emphasis theirs). "The research evidence shows that when students have prepared well for an examination, the number of students who gain by changing answers is significantly greater than the number of students who lose by changing answers."[29]

The key phrase is "prepared well." If you've studied well for the test, your second thought may be more apt to be correct.

HANDLING TRUE/FALSE QUESTIONS *True/false questions* **are statements that you must indicate are either "true" or "false."** Consequently, you have a 50 percent chance of getting each one right just by guessing. Instructors may therefore try to put in statements that *seem* true but on close reading actually are not. Here are some strategies for handling true/false questions:

- *Don't waste a lot of time.* Go through the true/false items as quickly as you can. Don't spend time agonizing over those you don't know; they usually aren't worth a lot of points compared with other parts of the test. Moreover, later questions may jog your memory in a way that suggests the correct answers.
- *Be aware that more answers are apt to be true than false.* True/false tests generally contain more true answers than false ones. Thus, mark a statement true unless you know for sure it is false.
- *Be aware longer statements tend to be true.* Statements that are longer and provide a lot of information tend to be true, though not always. Read the statement carefully to be sure no part of it is false.
- *Read carefully to see that every part is true.* For a statement to be true, *every* part of it must be true. Conversely, it is false if *any* part of it is false. (*Example:* "The original Thirteen Colonies included Massachusetts, Virginia, and Illinois" is a false statement because the last state was not among the thirteen, though the first two were.)
- *Look for qualifier words.* Qualifier words include *all, none, always, never, everyone, no one, invariably, rarely, often, usually, generally, sometimes, most.* Two suggestions to follow are these:
  1. Statements that use *absolute* qualifier words, such as "always" or "never," are usually false. (*Example:* "It's always dry in Nevada" is false because it does rain there sometimes.)
  2. Statements that use *moderating* qualifier words, such as "usually" or "often," tend to be true more often than not. (*Example:* "It's generally dry in Nevada" is true.)

HANDLING MULTIPLE-CHOICE QUESTIONS *Multiple-choice questions* **allow you to pick an answer from several options offered, generally between three and five choices.** The question itself is called the *stem*. The choices of answers are called the *options*. Incorrect options are known as *distractors* because their purpose is to distract you from choosing the correct option. Usually only one option is correct, but check the test directions (or ask the instructor) to see if more than one answer is allowed.

Two kinds of strategies apply to multiple-choice questions—*thinking strategies* and *guessing strategies*. Here are some thinking strategies:

- *Answer the question in your head first.* Read the question and try to frame an answer in your mind before looking at the answer options. This will help you avoid being confused by distractor options.

- *Eliminate incorrect answers first.* Read all the options. Sometimes two may be similar, with only one being correct. (Beware of trick answers that are only partly correct.) Eliminate those options you *know* are incorrect. Then choose the correct answer from those remaining.
- *Return to questions that are difficult.* Mark questions that are difficult and return to them later if time permits. Spending time mulling over multiple-choice questions may not pay off in the points allowed per question. Moreover, later questions in the test may trigger a line of thought that helps you with answers when you come back.
- *Try out each option independently with the question.* If you're having trouble sorting out the options, try reading the question and just the first option together. Then try the question and the second option together. And so on. By taking each one at a time, you may be able to make a better determination.
- *Be careful about "all of the above" or "none of the above."* "All of the above" or "none of the above" is often the correct choice. But examine the alternatives carefully. Make sure that *all* the other options apply before checking "all of the above." Make sure *no one other option* is correct before marking "none of the above."
- *Look for opposite choices.* If two choices are opposite in meaning, one is probably correct. Try to eliminate other choices, then concentrate on which of the opposing options is correct.

Here are some *guessing strategies* for multiple-choice questions:

- *Guess, if there's no penalty.* Unless the instructor will deduct points for incorrect answers, you might as well guess if you don't know the answer.
- *Choose between similar-sounding options.* If two options have similar words or similar-sounding words, choose one of them.
- *If options are numbers, pick in the middle.* If the alternative options consist of numbers, high and low numbers tend to be distractors. Thus, you might try guessing at one of the middle numbers.
- *Consider that the first option is often not correct.* Many instructors think you should have to read through at least one incorrect answer before you come to the correct answer. Thus, when guessing, consider the high probability that the first option will be incorrect.
- *Pick a familiar term over an unfamiliar one.* An answer that contains an unfamiliar term is apt to be a distractor, although many students tend to assume otherwise. If you have to guess, try the familiar term.

As with true/false questions, when you go back and review your answers, don't be afraid to change your mind if you realize that you could have made a better choice. The idea that you should always stick with your first choice is simply a myth.

HANDLING MATCHING QUESTIONS   _Matching questions_ **require you to associate items from one list with items from a second list.** For example, on a history test you might be asked to associate eight famous political figures listed in Column A with the time period in which each lived, as listed in Column B.

Strategies for handling matching questions are as follows:

- ***Ask if items can be used more than once.*** With most matching tests, each item in one column has its unique match in the other column. However, it's possible that items can be used for more than one match. That is, an item in Column B may fit several items in Column A. If you're not sure, ask the instructor.
- ***Read all choices before answering, then do the easy matchings first.*** Before making your choices, read all options in both columns. Then work the easy items first. Matching the easier items first may help you match the tougher ones later by a process of elimination.

If you can use an item only once, cross off each item as you use it. (If items can be used more than once, put a check mark next to the ones you have used rather than crossing them out.)

Put a question mark next to the matchings you're not sure about. If time permits, you can go back later and take another look at them.

HANDLING FILL-IN-THE-BLANK QUESTIONS   Also known as *"sentence-completion questions," **fill-in-the-blank questions** require you to fill in an answer from memory*. Often the answers are names, definitions, locations, amounts, or short descriptions. Frequently, clues within the incomplete sentence will help you with your answer.

Strategies for working fill-in-the-blank tests are as follows:

- ***Read the question to determine what kind of answer is needed.*** Reading the question carefully will tell you what kind of fact is needed: a key term? a date? a name? a definition? By focusing on the question, you may be able to trigger an association from your memory bank.
- ***Make sure the answer fits grammatically and logically.*** Be sure that subject and verb, plurals, numbers, and so on are used grammatically and logically. For example, if the statement says "a ____," don't put in "hour" and if it says "an ____," don't put in "minute." "A hour" and "An minute" are not grammatical.

As suggested for other types of objective questions, put a star or question mark beside those items you're not sure about. Later material on the test may prompt your memory when you come back to review them.

MASTERING WRITTEN EXAMINATIONS: SHORT & LONG ESSAY TESTS

Written examinations generally require you to write essays, either short or long. Both types of essays may be on the same exam.

- **Short-answer essay: A _short-answer essay_ may be a brief one-sentence answer to a short-answer question, a one- or two-paragraph**

essay, or a list or diagram. Usually you are asked to write a response to just one question.

- *Long-answer essay:* **A** <u>*long-answer essay*</u> **generally requires three or more paragraphs to answer.** You may be required to answer one question or several questions, all in the same essay.

Let's consider strategies for both of these.

The Short-Answer Essay

These questions require only a short answer—anywhere from a single sentence to two or three paragraphs. Examples are:

> *State the name of a particular theory.* (This might be a one-sentence answer.)
> *Define a certain term.* (This might require a sentence or two.)
> *List the basic steps in a process.* (This could be several sentences or a list.)
> *Describe a particular scientific study.* (This might require a paragraph.)
> *Identify and describe three causes of a particular event.* (This might be done in two or three paragraphs.)

Your strategy here is to provide the instructor with enough information (but not too much) to show that you understand the answer—whether it's a list, some brief sentences, or a few paragraphs.

How much detail should you provide? This is sometimes difficult to determine. After all, identifying and describing three causes of World War I could take several pages. To decide how much detail is appropriate, consider three factors:

- *Time available:* How much time do you have for other questions on the exam? You may need to allow for an upcoming long-essay question, for example.
- *Point value:* What is the relative weight (number of points) the instructor assigns to short-answer questions compared with other questions?
- *Your knowledge:* How much do you know about the topic? The instructor might mark you down if you volunteer erroneous information.

In general, it's best to write the minimum you think necessary. If in doubt, respond to one short-answer question, then take it up to the instructor and ask if it's long enough.

Handling the Long-Answer Essay

The long-answer essay (and to some extent the short-answer essay) is sometimes considered a *subjective* test. This notion would seem to imply there are no objective facts and that it's entirely up to the grader to determine how good your answer is. Actually, there usually are objective facts that the instructor will look for in your answer.

In handling the long-answer essay, you'll be demonstrating not only the lower-order critical-thinking skills (identified by Bloom) of *memorization* and *compre-*

hension, but also the higher-order critical-thinking skills of *application, analysis, synthesis,* and *evaluation.* Recall what these mean:

Memorization: "I can recognize and recall the information."
Comprehension: "I can recall information in my own terms and explain them to a friend."
Application: "I can apply what I've learned in a new area."
Analysis: "I can break apart these ideas and relate them to other concepts."
Synthesis: "I can build on other knowledge to put together the elements to form a new whole."
Evaluation: "I can use all these thinking skills to form a judgment."

What strategy should you follow on a long-answer question? According to one clinical psychologist and instructor of first-year seminar courses, research shows that instructors award the greatest number of points when an essay answer meets the following six standards:[30]

1. *Relevance:* The answer sticks to the question. That is, the facts and points set down are relevant to the question.
2. *Completeness:* The question is answered completely.
3. *Accuracy:* The information given is factually correct.
4. *Organization:* The answer is organized well.
5. *Logic:* The answer shows that the writer can think and reason effectively.
6. *Clarity:* Thoughts are expressed clearly.

Basically, then, two things are important in answering essay questions. First, you need to know your facts. Second you need to present them well.

Let's now outline a strategy for answering long-answer essay questions.

READ THE DIRECTIONS!   This is important for all test questions, of course, but especially here, because of the amount of time you're required to invest in responding to long-answer essay questions and the high point values attached to them.

In failing to read the directions carefully, students may answer only one question when three have been asked. Or they may answer three when only one has been asked (thereby depriving themselves of time to respond adequately to later test questions). Or they may go off on a tangent with an answer that earns no credit. As instructors, we don't know how many times we've written in the margins of tests, "Nice response, but it misses the point. Did you read the directions?"

Reading the directions will help you stay on the topic, thereby helping you to meet Standard 1 above—making the answer *relevant.*

LOOK FOR GUIDING WORDS IN THE DIRECTIONS   When you read the directions, look for guiding words—key task words such as "discuss," "define," or "compare"—which may guide your answer. **<u>Guiding words</u> define the task you are to accomplish in your essay-question answer.**

Common guiding words are *analyze, compare, contrast, criticize, define, describe, discuss, enumerate, explain, evaluate, illustrate, interpret, outline, prove, relate, state, summarize,* and *trace.*

As you read the directions, circle or underline the guiding words so that you know exactly what is required of you. This will help you achieve Standards 2 and 3—making your answer *complete* and *accurate.*

IF YOU HAVE A CHOICE OF ESSAY QUESTIONS, READ THEM ALL
Some tests will allow you to choose which of, say, two or three essay questions you want to answer. In order to take your best shot, read *all* such questions, circling the guiding words. Then pick the essay question you think you can answer best.

BRAINSTORM IDEAS   Now it's time to go to work by doing some brainstorming. It's best to make your notes on a separate sheet of scratch paper. (If you use a part of the exam-questions sheet or blue book, be sure to cross them out afterward. You don't want to confuse the grader and have your notes figured into your point values—unless you're attaching the outline because you've run out of writing time.)
     Here's how to proceed:

1. *Brainstorm***, which means jot down all the ideas that come to mind in response to the directions in the question.** Just blow out as many ideas as you can that seem to be pertinent. Do this for a minute or two. This will help ensure that you haven't left anything out—helping you to achieve Standard 2, *completeness.*
2. Next, read through your notes and *underline the important ideas.* These will become the basis for your outline and your essay.

MAKE AN OUTLINE OF YOUR PROSPECTIVE ANSWER   At this point you may feel under extreme pressure to simply begin writing. However, by taking another minute to make an outline you will help achieve Standard 4—your answer will be *organized.*
     Many students find that a certain formula for an outline seems to help them organize their thoughts and touch on the main points of the answer. The outline formula consists of three parts—Your Position, Supporting Details, and Summary:

Part 1, *Your Position,* states your position or viewpoint in response to the question being asked. It says what you are going to write about.
Part 2, *Supporting Details,* lists the supporting evidence for your position. These might be three or more facts. In your outline, jot down key words that represent these facts.
Part 3, *Summary,* restates your position. It may include an additional supporting "minifact."

One reason for making an outline is that, if you run out of time and can't finish, you can attach the outline to your test answer and get partial credit.

WRITE YOUR ESSAY   Let's show how the essay-writing process works.

- *Do Part 1, Your Position, by writing the first paragraph, which rewrites or restates the test question, states your position, and lists the evidence.* If you follow the above formula for the first paragraph, you will show your instructor that you are achieving Standard 5—your answer is *logical*.

1. In the first sentence, include part of the examination question in your answer (without using the exact same words the instructor used). This will help you overcome inertia or anxiety and get going.
2. Next, state the position or point of view you will take.
3. Then list, in sentence form, the facts you will discuss as evidence to support your position, starting with the strongest points in order to make a good impression.

- **Do Part 2, Supporting Details, by expanding each fact into a paragraph.** Now you take the supporting facts you stated in sentence form in the first paragraph and address each one separately. Expand each fact into a full paragraph with supporting details. Use transitional sentences to connect the supporting details so that the reader can follow the progress of your discussion.
- **Do Part 3, Summary, by writing a paragraph summarizing your position and adding a supporting minifact.** The conclusion is basically a summary paragraph in which you simply restate your position. If you have an additional supporting minifact (or a supporting detail you've forgotten until now), this can punch up your ending a bit and bring your essay to a dramatic close.

MAKE SURE YOUR ESSAY IS CLEAR   Here are some tips to help you achieve Standard 6—*clarity*.

1. *Write legibly,* in pen rather than pencil (which is difficult to read), and write neatly rather than in a frantic scrawl. Because grading of essay questions is somewhat subjective, avoid irritating the instructor by making your answer hard to read.
2. *Write on one side of the paper only.* Writing on both sides allows the ink to show through. Writing on one side also leaves you the opposite side of the page as a place to write an insert later in case you've forgotten something.
3. *Leave generous space between paragraphs and in the margin.* Leaving space gives you an opportunity to add material later in such a way that you don't have to cram it in and make it hard to read.
4. *Proofread.* If you have time, go back over your answer and check for grammar, spelling, and legibility in order to boost the clarity of your effort.

WATCH YOUR TIME   Throughout the test you should keep track of your time, periodically checking to see how much time you have left. Answer the easy questions first to build confidence, but after that give more time to questions that are worth more points.

When we were students ourselves, we thought successful test taking was often a matter of luck or having some sort of inherited smarts. However, you can see from the foregoing that it's pretty much a learned skill. And there's no question you're capable of learning it.

How to Write a Successful Term Paper

CHAPTER
5

Think about the meaning of the word *term* in *term paper*. Doing the paper is supposed to take the greater part of a school term—that is, a semester or quarter. Thus, **a _term paper_ is supposed to be a paper based on extensive research of a specific subject and include proper documentation**. When finished it should probably run 10 or more double-spaced pages done on a word processor (equivalent to about 20 handwritten pages). Because so much effort is required, no wonder instructors often consider the term paper to be worth *50 percent* of the course grade. This suggests why it's worth giving it your best shot, instead of just knocking it out over a weekend (equivalent to cramming for a test).

What Do Instructors Look for in a Term Paper?

Perhaps the best way to get oriented is to ask, "How do instructors grade term papers?" These are probably the three principal standards:[1]

- Demonstration of originality and effort
- Demonstration that learning took place
- Neatness, correctness, and appearance of the presentation

DEMONSTRATION OF ORIGINALITY AND EFFORT Are the ideas in your paper original, and does the paper show some effort? Instructors are constantly on the lookout for papers that do not represent students' own thoughts and efforts. These papers can take three forms, ranging from most serious (and dangerous to the student) to least serious:

- *"Canned" or lifted papers:* Canned papers are those bought from Internet or other commercial term-paper-writing services or rewritten or lifted from old papers written by others.

    Beware of submitting a paper that is not your own. The instructor might recognize it as the work of a student who was there before you or suspect the style is not yours. If you're found out, you'll not only flunk the course but probably will be put on some form of academic probation. This means you might be suspended or expelled from school.

- *Plagiarized papers:* The ideas or expressions in a paper are ***plagiarized* if they are another person's passed off as one's own**—if you've copied passages from another source without giving credit to the source, for instance.

  Most instructors have particular sensitivity to plagiarism. They can tell when the level of thought or expression does not seem appropriate for student writing. Moreover, lifting others' ideas goes against the fundamental reason you're in school to begin with: to learn ways to meet challenges and expand your competence. In any case, plagiarism can also result in a failing grade in the course and possible suspension from school.

- *Unoriginal, no-effort papers:* Quite often students submit papers that *show no thought and effort.* They consist of simply quoting and citing—that is, rehashing—the conflicting ideas of various experts and scholars. There is no evidence that the student has weighed the various views and demonstrated some critical thinking. A 10-page paper that shows original thinking is always better than a 20-page paper with lots of footnotes but no insights of your own.

DEMONSTRATION THAT LEARNING TOOK PLACE Instructors want you to demonstrate that you've learned something—the very reason you're supposed to be in school in the first place.

How do you show that you're learning? Our suggestion: Ask a question for which the term paper provides the answer. Examples of questions are as follows:

Do men and women view date rape differently?
Are alcohol and cigarettes really gateway drugs to illegal drug use?
What's the best way to dispose of radioactive waste?

Always try, if you can, to make the question one that's important or interesting to you. That way you'll be genuinely motivated to learn something from the answer. At the end of your paper, you'll be able to demonstrate that learning took place. For example, you might conclude: "When I first looked into the question of date rape, I wondered whether men and women view the matter differently. As the research in this paper has shown, I have found that . . ."

NEATNESS, CORRECTNESS, AND APPEARANCE OF PRESENTATION
Like most readers, instructors prefer neatness over messiness, readability over unreadability. Studies show that instructors give higher grades to papers that are neat and use correct spelling and grammar. The third standard, then, involves form. Is your paper typed and proofread? Does it follow the correct form for footnotes and references? Does it have a title page?

Consider these points:

- *Typed versus handwritten:* All instructors *prefer*—and many require—that your paper be produced on a word processor or a typewriter rather than handwritten. Even if you're only a hunt-and-peck typist, try to render the final version of your term paper on a word processor or typewriter. Or hire someone else to type it.

- *Correct spelling and grammar:* As you write, look up words in the dictionary to check their spelling. Proofread the final version to correct any mistakes and bad grammar. If you're using a word processor, run the final draft through spell-checker and grammar-checking programs—and also read it over yourself, because those programs won't catch everything.

    You may be sick and tired of your paper when you finally get done with it. Nevertheless, you would hate to blow it at the end by allowing the instructor to mark it down because you overlooked the small stuff.
- *Correct academic form:* Different academic disciplines (English and psychology, for example) have their preferred footnote and works-cited styles. Be sure to follow any directions your instructor gives for these and any other requirements for the form of the paper.

Now you know what you're aiming for. Let's see how to achieve it.

WRITING A TERM PAPER: FIVE PHASES

The audience for a term paper is your instructor. In this section we explain the five principal phases of preparing a term paper for an instructor:

Phase 1: Picking a topic
Phase 2: Doing initial research and developing a preliminary outline
Phase 3: Doing further research—using the library
Phase 4: Sorting your notes, revising the outline, and writing a first draft
Phase 5: Revising, typing, and proofreading your paper—employing critical thinking

Be aware that the grade on your term paper will count heavily toward your grade in the course. Thus, you should spread these phases over the semester or quarter—not do them all in one week or a few days. Clearly, time management is important.

Phase 1: Picking a Topic

Students often procrastinate on this first step. However, the most important advice we can give you about writing papers is: *Start early.* By beginning early, you'll be able to find a topic that interests you. Moreover, you'll avoid pitfalls such as picking a subject that is too narrow or too large.

SET A DEADLINE FOR PICKING YOUR TOPIC　Set this deadline as soon as you get your instructor's guidelines for the term paper. In your lecture notes, on a page by itself, write a big note to yourself:

°°° DEADLINE: PICK TERM PAPER TOPIC BY TUESDAY NOON! °°°

In addition, put this on your to-do list and your weekly planner.

PICK A TOPIC: TWO CRITERIA　Pick something that is (1) important to your instructor and (2) interesting to you.

- *Topics important to the instructor:* You need to determine what is important to your instructor, because he or she is the sole audience for your paper.

     How do you find out what the instructor believes is significant? First, if he or she has provided written guidelines, read them carefully. If the assignment is given verbally, take precise notes. You'll also get a better idea of what's important when you meet with the instructor to discuss your proposed topics.
- *Topics interesting to you:* Motivation is everything. Whenever possible, try to choose a topic that interests you. It also helps if you already know something about it. To determine what might be suitable, look through your lecture notes and textbook to see what pops out at you. You can communicate with the instructor to explore topic ideas.

EXPRESS PROPOSED TOPICS AS THREE QUESTIONS   By the time your self-imposed deadline arrives for choosing your topic, you should have three alternative ideas. Because your purpose is to demonstrate that you're learning, these should be expressed as questions.

For example, for an introductory health course, you may decide on the following possible topics.

> *What diets are most effective for weight loss?*
> *Does meditation prolong life in cancer patients?*
> *Does wearing helmets reduce motorcycle injuries?*

Are some of these questions too broad (diets) or too narrow (helmets)? In the next step, you'll find out.

CHECK TOPIC IDEAS WITH YOUR INSTRUCTOR   It's now a good idea (in fact, you may be required) to discuss your topic questions with your instructor. Questions to ask are the following:

- *Is it important enough?* Ask your instructor, "Do you think any of these topics are important enough to be worth exploring in a term paper?" The answer will indicate whether you are meeting the first criterion in selecting a topic—does the instructor think it's significant?
- *Is the scope about right?* Ask, "Do you think the topic is too broad or too narrow in scope?" The instructor may suggest ways to limit or vary the topic so you won't waste time on unnecessary research. He or she can also prevent you from tackling a topic that's too advanced. Equally important, the instructor may be able to suggest books or other resources that will help you in your research.

Phase 2: Doing Initial Research & Developing an Outline

Once your topic is chosen, you can begin researching your topic and drafting an outline. If Phase 1 took you one week, it should take you another week to do Phase 2. Here, too, you should write a big note to yourself (and put it on your weekly calendar and to-do list):

*** DEADLINE: CHECK OUT RESEARCH FOR TERM PAPER BY WED. 5 P.M.! ***

The idea here is to satisfy yourself about two things:

1. *Research material:* Is enough material available to you so that you can adequately research your paper?
2. *Rough outline:* Do you have a rough idea of the direction your paper will take?

INVESTIGATING RESEARCH MATERIAL   This step need not take long—perhaps a half hour. You can do it with online searches or at a library. The idea is to look in a handful of places to get a sense of the research material available to you. Here are two possibilities:

- *Library online catalog:* Look under the subject listing in the library's online catalog to see what books exist on your topic. (We explain the online catalog on page 98.) Don't assume, however, that just because the books are listed that they are easily available. They may be checked out, on reserve, or in another campus library. An online catalog may tell you if they're checked out. Look up some call letters for relevant titles, then visit the shelves and see what books you can find.

    Note: If you need to get books through interlibrary loan, allow 7–10 days before the books are in hand.
- *Guide to periodicals:* Magazines and journals are apt to be more up to date than books. In the library, check the *Reader's Guide to Periodical Literature* to see what articles are available in your topic area. Jot down the names of the periodicals, then check with the reference librarian to see if they are available. Or check such library computerized databases as DataTimes, DIALOG, ERIC, InfoTrac® College Edition, LEXIS/NEXIS, OCLC, or VU/TEXT.

Further information about the library is given in Phase 3, Research. This preliminary investigation is simply to give you an overview of the subject. (If your preliminary investigation shows few resources, you'll need to go back quickly to Phase 1 and consult with your instructor about another possible topic.)

DEVELOPING AN OUTLINE   While you're doing your first research, you should also do a preliminary outline. The purpose of doing a preliminary outline now is twofold: First, it saves you time later; second, it provides you with a general road map. You can always change the outline later. But if you start without one, you may waste time before you get a sense of direction.

Take a sheet of paper and write OUTLINE #1 across the top. Then fill in the following three parts—I. Beginning, II. Middle, and III. End.[2]

Following are the general functions of each part:

I. Beginning—The Introduction. This part describes the one or two main questions your paper will try to answer. In the final paper, the beginning will be one or two paragraphs.

Examples: "How smart are college athletes? Are college athletics dominated by 'dumb jocks'?"

II. Middle—The Body. This portion of the outline describes specific questions your paper will try to answer. These detailed questions help you answer the main questions.

Examples: "What's the grade-point average (GPA) of college football, baseball, and basketball players? What's the GPA of competitive swimmers, gymnasts, and tennis players? What percentage of athletes graduate compared to other students? What percentage drop out? What proportion of athletes in pro sports are college graduates? Are top athletes usually top scholars, such as Phi Beta Kappa, magna cum laude, Rhodes Scholars?" And so on.

III. End—The Conclusion. You won't know the end or conclusion, of course, until you've done the research and answered your questions. For now, just state that you will write a conclusion based on your answers.

Here are some techniques for developing the outline for your particular topic:

1. **Write questions on index cards.** Get a stack of 3″ × 5″ index cards or cut sheets of notepaper into quarters. On each card or quarter-page, write a question you want to answer about your topic. *Write as many questions as you can think of, both general and detailed.* (You can also type these questions, using your word processor, of course.)

2. **Organize index cards into categories.** Now sort your 3″ × 5″ cards into stacks by category. One stack might contain a few general questions that will make up your introduction; the others could be categorized according to the body of the outline.

   What categories might you have? Some stacks may be of similar kinds of questions. Some might be advantages and disadvantages, causes and effects, or comparisons and contrasts. Do whatever kind of grouping seems sensible to you.

3. **Write out your outline.** Copy the categories and questions into the outline form shown above. You now have a road map to follow to begin your research.

   Note: Rather than 3″ × 5″ cards, you may find an outlining program (available with your word processing program) more useful. This kind of software allows you to brainstorm and sort out ideas onscreen.

After developing your outline, e-mail it or show it to your instructor. He or she will be able to determine at a glance whether you seem to be headed in the right direction.

Phase 3: Doing Your Research

Phase 3 consists of making use of the library or online resources to do your research.

"The *library!*" you may say. "Why bother when there's the Internet?"

For students who grew up with the World Wide Web, the idea of using the library just seems like too much effort. Yet if you don't know advanced Web-searching techniques, a simple online search for, say, information about the planet Mars can produce tens of thousands of hits (references). It may take an hour and a half to find something online that could quickly be found in a library. "What bothers me most," says Christine Borgman, chair of the UCLA Department of Library and Information Science, "is that computer people seem to think that if you have access to the Web, you don't need libraries."[3] But what's in a library is standardized and well organized, whereas what's on the Web is often overwhelming, unstandardized, and chaotic.

HOW TO FIND WHAT YOU WANT IN BOOKS   Books may be found on open shelves in the main section of the library. In some places, they may also be in the "stacks," requiring a library page or runner to go get them. Or they may be in special libraries located elsewhere on campus, such as those attached to the business school or the law school. Or they may be available by means of ***interlibrary loan,* a service that enables you to borrow books from other libraries.** Allow extra time—several days or a week or so—and perhaps expect to pay a small fee when obtaining a book through interlibrary loan.

One way to find books that may be helpful to you is to go to the *Books in Print.* This is an annual reference work—organized by title, author, and subject— that lists most books currently in print in the United States. By using the subject category you can also find books in your area of research, although they won't necessarily be in your school's library.

The way to find a book in your particular library is to use the library's ***online catalog*—a computerized list of all the books available at the library—** which in most places has replaced the card catalog consisting of file drawers of file cards. Online catalogs require that you use a computer terminal or microcomputer that has a wired connection to a database. The instructions for using online catalogs appear on the computer keyboard or on the display screen (in Help screens). An advantage of online catalogs is that you can use key words to search for material by title, author, or subject. ***Key words* are words you use to find specific information.** For example, you could use the key words "National Socialism" to look for books about Hitler and the Nazi Party.

Most schools' libraries use the Library of Congress system of call numbers and letters. Get the call numbers from the card or computerized catalog, then use a map of the library to find the appropriate shelves. Once you've found your book, look at other books in the general vicinity to see if they could be useful.

If you can't find a book on the shelves and decide you really need it, ask a librarian for help. It may be in the reference section or on reserve for a class. If it has been checked out, ask the library to put a hold on it for you when it's returned. Or ask for help getting another copy through interlibrary loan.

HOW TO FIND WHAT YOU WANT IN NEWSPAPERS, MAGAZINES, AND JOURNALS   You can see what general newspapers, magazines, and journals are available by simply looking at the open shelves in the periodicals reading room. A list of the library's holdings in periodicals should also be available at the main desk. Finally, some online catalogs also provide information regarding periodicals.

Here are some printed and online avenues for finding articles in the research area you're interested in. Indexes to periodicals appear in the library's reference section.

- ***Newspaper indexes:*** In the United States, the newspapers available nationally and in many campus libraries are the *New York Times,* the *Wall Street Journal,* and *USA Today.* Some schools may also subscribe to other respected newspapers, such as the *Washington Post* or the *Los Angeles Times.* Some newspapers print indexes that list information about the articles appearing in their pages. Examples are the *New York Times Index* and the *Wall Street Journal Index.* Look also for *Newspaper Abstracts* and *Editorials on File.*

  In addition, your library may subscribe to computerized databases providing bibliographical information about articles appearing in hundreds of magazines and newspapers. Ask the librarian how you can use *DataTimes, DIALOG,* or the reference services of *America Online, CompuServe, Microsoft Network, Prodigy,* or *NEXIS.*

- ***Magazine indexes:*** The index for the 100 or so most general magazines, many probably available in your library, is the *Readers' Guide to Periodical Literature.* This lists articles appearing in such well-known magazines as *Time, Newsweek, Reader's Digest,* and *Psychology Today.*

  Other indexes, available in printed, microfilm, or CD-ROM form, are *Magazine Index, Newsbank, InfoTrac College Edition, Business Index,* and *Medline.*

- ***Journal indexes and abstracts:*** Journals are specialized magazines, and their articles are listed in specialized indexes and databases. Examples range from *Applied Science* and *Technology Index* to *Social Science Index.*

  In addition, there are indexes to ***abstracts*****, which are paragraphs summarizing articles along with bibliographical information about them**. Examples range from *Biological Abstracts* to *Sociological Abstracts.*

  Some journal indexes are accessed by going online through a computer. For example, PsycLit is a bibliographic database to Psychological Abstracts, scholarly articles in psychology.

HOW TO FIND OTHER LIBRARY REFERENCE MATERIALS   Among other wonderful reference materials available are these:

- ***Dictionaries, thesauruses, style books:*** Need to look up specialized terms for your paper? The reference section of the library has not only standard dictionaries but also specialized dictionaries for technical subjects. Examples range from *Dictionary of Biological Sciences* to *Webster's New World Dictionary of Computer Terms.*

  In addition, you may find a thesaurus helpful in your writing. A ***thesaurus*** **lists synonyms, or words with similar meanings**. This is a great resource when you can't think of the exact word you want when writing. Many computers now come with a thesaurus built in.

  Finally, various style books are available to help you create tables, footnotes, and bibliographies, such as *The Chicago Manual of Style* and *The American Psychological Association Style Manual.*

- *Encyclopedias, almanacs, handbooks:* No doubt the library has various kinds of standard encyclopedias, in printed and CD-ROM form. As with dictionaries, there are also encyclopedias on specialized subjects. Examples range from *Cyclopedia of World Authors* to *The Wellness Encyclopedia.*

  You can also find all kinds of specialized almanacs, handbooks, and other reference sources. Examples range from *The Business Writer's Handbook* to *The Secret Guide to Computers.*

  Nowadays there are a number of encyclopedias available as software. Examples of CD-ROM reference works are *Eyewitness History of the World, Eyewitness Encyclopedia of Nature, Skier's Encyclopedia,* and *The Way Things Work.* You can get the full text of 1,750 great works of literature and other books and documents on Library of the Future.

- *Government literature:* A section of the library is probably reserved for information from both the federal government and state and local governments. The most prolific publisher in the world is the United States government. To find out publications pertinent to your subject, look in *The Monthly Catalog* and *PAIS (Public Affairs Information Service).*

GET ONLINE RESEARCH HELP   Chapter 2 described the use of online search engines (such as AltaVista or HotBot) and online subject catalogs (such as Yahoo! or Excite). In this and the next few sections, we review some other sources. (Online sources, of course, need to be documented just like a book or periodical.)

Following are some initial questions to consider if you need online research help:

- *Can I access online library information from home?* Some electronic databases restrict the number of users allowed. This may mean that users can't access those databases unless they are able to walk into the library, have a computer account with that library, are enrolled in a college course (even an extension course), or have a special corporate account that allows them access.

- *Can I download information I find in the library?* You might find that you can access a library's online catalog from home, but you may not be able to download material electronically. Even so, you might be able to visit the library to obtain materials you need. Or librarians may be able to ship materials to you. Or you may be able to ask your nearby local public library to get the materials via the interlibrary loan system. (Be sure to allow enough time—perhaps 7–10 days.) Or perhaps the library in question will provide photocopies of articles.

- *How can I get help over the phone from a reference librarian?* If you have a particular question that goes beyond the knowledge of the part-timers or students who often work in a library, telephone the library (the phone number may be listed on the library's Website, if it has one) and find out how to get help from a reference librarian. He or she may be able to help you locate special materials, such as maps, statistics, or special government documents.

USE INTERNET-BASED REFERENCE INFORMATION AND LIBRARY CATALOGS   With Internet access, you can connect with the online catalog of your school, (perhaps) your local public library, and with reference information and the online catalogs of libraries all over the world. Some libraries even make their collections accessible online. Or you can browse through the catalog to discover what you want, then get the book or document sent to you through interlibrary loan or through an article photocopy request.

Try the following:

- *The Internet Public Library:* The Reference Center home page of the Internet Public Library (*www.ipl.org/ref*), a project of the School of Information at the University of Michigan, shows a picture (called an "image map") of a lobby or reception area. You click on the picture of the desk if you want to ask a reference question. You click on a picture of a book (such as Social Sciences or Education) to get information within a particular area. Incidentally, the IPL site also features a section on how to write a paper without going nuts.
- *Encyclopedia.com:* Based on the *Concise Columbia Electronic Encyclopedia,* Encyclopedia.com (*www.encyclopedia.com*) offers more than 50,000 short articles, plus links to millions of articles and pictures in Electric Library.
- *Libdex—library catalogs on the World Wide Web:* Libdex, short for the Library Index, is found at *www.libdex.com.* Libdex is a worldwide directory of 17,000 library home pages. You can use your browser to search the index in two ways—by country and by OPAC vendor.

  If you click on *Country,* you can search by country, then state, then by type of library. For instance, if you click your mouse on *USA,* then click on *Nevada,* you will get a list of seven types of libraries: academic (colleges and universities); public; government; law; consortia (groups of libraries that band together, such as the Las Vegas – Clark County Library District); the U.S. State Library; and special libraries (the Desert Research Institute). If you click on, say, *University of Nevada—Reno library,* you will get access to the library's home page and Web catalog.

  The other choice, *OPAC,* stands for Online Public Access Catalog. Clicking on this will yield a list of worldwide libraries that post their holdings online. If you then click on, say, *OCLC* (Online Computer Library Center), you will get a list of indexes in the United States and Canada, one of which— say, the Silicon Valley Library System—will lead you to a cooperative system of public libraries—in this case, in Santa Clara County, California.
- *Use Telnet to access OPAC:* Some OPACs are searchable on the Web, but others can only be accessed using **_Telnet_, a text-based protocol that predates the Web.** Both Windows and Macintosh computers come with Telnet application software (called a "Telnet client") for making the necessary connections, as do most browsers. Telnet is not point-and-click, as Web-based programs are. Instead it features command-driven menus. You may need Telnet software for accessing some of the smaller libraries or for connecting from university libraries to other sites.

- ***The Library of Congress—America's national library:*** The Library of Congress (located at *lcweb.loc.gov*) contains more than 17 million books and 111 million other items. Once you're at the Library of Congress home page, you can go to the bottom of the screen to Help & FAQs to orient yourself. If you know what you're looking for, you can click on Search the Catalog at the top of the screen.

In addition, many libraries subscribe to computerized information networks, such as DIALOG, ERIC, ORBIT, and BSR. Directories and guides exist to help you learn to use these services. Examples are *Directory of Online Databases, Encyclopedia of Information Systems and Services,* and *Guide to the Use of Libraries and Information Services.*

LOW-TECH WAYS TO COLLECT INFORMATION AT A LIBRARY   Some materials (principally books) you'll be able to check out and use at your usual writing desk. However, most libraries won't let you take out magazines, encyclopedias, and general reference materials. Thus, you'll need to be able to take notes in the library.

Traditional 3″ × 5″ index cards are useful because you can write one idea on each card, then later sort the cards as you please. Index cards should be used in three ways—as source cards, information cards, and idea cards.

Source Cards. Use these to keep track of bibliographical information. At the time you're looking up your sources, you can jot down the call letters on these cards. Once you find the source, you can copy information you'll need for your bibliography, specifically:

- For each *journal article,* write down the author's last and first name (for example, "Wahlstrom, Carl"), title of article, title of journal, month and year, volume and issue number, and page numbers.
- For each *book,* write down the author's (or editor's) name, book title, edition, city and state of publication, name of publisher, year of publication (listed on the copyright page), and pages you referred to, if necessary.

Later, when you type your references, you'll be able to arrange these source cards in alphabetical order by authors' last names, as follows:

Wahlstrom, C., & Williams, B. K. (2002). *Learning success: Being your best at college & life.* Belmont, CA: Wadsworth.

Note: This reference follows APA (American Psychological Association) style. Your instructor may require that you use a different format.

Information Cards. Use information cards to copy down information and quotations. This is the actual research material you will use. The card will have three areas:

- ***Source abbreviation:*** At the top of each card, put an abbreviated version of the source, including the page number. (*Example:* "Wahlstrom 2002, p. 23."

If you have two 2002 Wahlstrom references, label them a and b.) If you use more than one card for a single source, number the cards.

- *Information:* In the lower part of the card, write the information. If it's a direct quote, enclose it in quotation marks so you'll be sure to add a citation (and avoid the appearance of plagiarism) when you write your paper.
- *Key-word zone:* Reserve the top right corner of the card for a "key-word zone." In this area put one or two key words that will tie the card to a place on your outline. (*Example:* "Graduation rates.") The key word can also tie the card to a new subject, if it is not on your current outline.

Idea Cards. Use these to jot down ideas that occur to you. To make sure you don't mix them up with information cards, write "IDEA #1," "IDEA #2," and so on, at the top.

To keep the cards organized, keep them in three separate stacks, each wrapped in a rubber band.

HIGH-TECH WAYS TO COLLECT INFORMATION AT A LIBRARY   Using 3″ × 5″ cards is a traditional, though low-tech, way to collect information. They can also be somewhat time-consuming, given that you must to write out everything by hand.

Two high-tech ways to collect information in the library are using photocopiers and portable computers:

- *Photocopiers:* When you find an article from which you'd like to quote extensively, it may make sense to simply use the library's photocopying machines. Sometimes this means feeding the machine a lot of dimes, but the time saving may still be worth it. Some libraries allow students to open charge accounts for use of these machines.

  For organizing purposes, you can then take scissors and cut up the photocopied material. Then write the source abbreviation and page number in one margin and the "key words" in the other.
- *Laptop computers:* Having a portable computer with a word processing program can be a godsend in collecting library information. (If your library has desktop word processors installed on the premises, you might also be able to use them.) Even if you're not very fast on the keyboard, it may still be faster than writing out your information by hand. Follow the same format as you would for 3″ × 5″ cards.

Be sure to collect complete source information (shown under "Source Cards" above) for each book and article from which you photocopy or type material.

WAYS TO COLLECT INFORMATION FROM ONLINE SOURCES   Even if you never set foot in a library, you can still get the information you want.

- *Download and print out information.* A great deal of the research material you find online can simply be downloaded from the Website and printed out on your computer printer at home. This is by far the most convenient way, but unfortunately a lot of material is not available this way. Some older material (such as that created before the 1980s) may not be available in online database form. Other material is, but the owners of the database (such as the *New York Times*) may want to charge you a fee for the download. If you're successful, check the required style manual for ways to document these sources.

- **Use interlibrary loan.** We've mentioned this already: You ask the library where you have borrowing privileges (such as the library of the school from which you're taking a distance learning course) to get a book, audiotape, videotape, or the like from another library.
- **Get a photocopy.** If you can't download an article or document, you can ask your librarian to send you a photocopy of it. You may be charged a small fee for this.
- **Use commercial document-delivery service.** Many businesses will, for a fee, find and photocopy articles on request. Examples are UnCover (*http://uncweb.carl.org*) and Information Express (*www.express.com*). Commercial document delivery services are listed on the Website of the Association of Independent Information Professionals (*www.aiip.org*).

Phase 4: Sorting Your Notes, Revising the Outline, & Writing the First Draft

The research phase may have taken a lot of work, but now it's time to put it all together.

ESTABLISH YOUR WRITING PLACE   What kind of writing environment suits you best is up to you. The main thing is that it help you avoid distractions. You may also need room to spread out, even be able to put $3'' \times 5''$ cards and sources on the floor. If you write in longhand or use a laptop, a table in the library may do. If you write on a typewriter, you may need to place a desk in your room.

Some other tips:

- **Allow time.** Give yourself plenty of time. A first draft of a major paper should take more than one day.
- **Reread instructions.** Just before you start to write, reread the instructor's directions regarding the paper. You would hate to find out afterward that you took the wrong approach because you overlooked something.

Ready? Begin.

SORT YOUR NOTES AND REVISE YOUR OUTLINE   When gathering your information, you may have been following the questions that appeared on your preliminary outline. However, the very process of doing research may turn up some new questions and areas that you hadn't thought of. Thus, your $3'' \times 5''$ cards or source materials may contain information that suggests some changes to the outline.

Here's what to do:

Sort Your Information Cards. Keeping your eye on the key words in the upper right corner of your 3″ × 5″ cards (or other source material), sort the information material into piles. *Each pile should contain information relating to a similar question or topic.* Now move the piles into the sequence in which you will discuss the material, according to your preliminary outline.

Revise Your Outline. The piles may suggest some changes in the order of your outline. Thus, you should now take a fresh sheet of paper, write *OUTLINE #2* at the top, and redo the questions or categories.

By now you will be able to write answers to some or all of your questions. *Do this as you rework the outline.* Refer to the sources of your information as you write. For example, suppose you have the question "What percentage of basketball players graduate compared to most students?" You might write "NCAA 1995 study: No breakdown by sports. However, at basketball Final Four schools, graduation rates were as follows: North Carolina 76% student-athletes, 48% all students; UCLA 56% and 77%; Arkansas 39% and 41%; Oklahoma State 38% and 40% (Anderson, p. B5)."

Resequence the topics so that they seem to follow logically, with one building on another.

Write a Thesis Statement and Working Title. When you get done with reworking and answering questions in *II. Middle of your outline,* go back up to *I. Beginning.* Revise the main question or questions into a ***thesis statement***—**this is a concise sentence that defines the purpose of your paper.** For example, your original main questions were "How smart are college athletes?" and "Are college athletics dominated by 'dumb jocks'?" These might now become the following thesis statement:

> Though graduation rates of college athletes are lower than those for other students, some individual athletes are among the best students.

The thesis statement will in turn suggest a ***working title***, **which is a tentative title for your paper.** Thus, you might put down on your outline:

> Working title: "How Smart Are College Athletes?"

WRITE YOUR FIRST DRAFT The first draft has one major purpose: *to get your ideas down on paper.* This is not the stage to worry about doing a clever introduction or choosing the right words or making transitions between ideas. Nor should you concern yourself about correct grammar, punctuation, and spelling. Simply write as though you were telling your findings to a friend. *It's important not to be too judgmental about your writing at this point.* Your main task is to get from a blank page to a page with *something* on it that you can refine later.

Proceed as follows:

Write the Middle. Skip the beginning, letting your thesis statement be the introduction for now. Instead, follow your revised outline (Outline #2) to create *II. Middle:* Write the body of your paper, using your information cards to flesh it out.

Set down your answers or ideas one after the other, without worrying too much about logical transitions between them. Use your own voice, not some imagined scholarly tone.

Follow some of the writing suggestions mentioned in the next section, "Some Writing Tips."

Write the Beginning. When you have finished setting down the answers to all the questions in the middle, go back and do *I. Beginning.* By starting with the middle, you'll avoid the hang-up of trying to get your paper off the ground or of writing an elegant lead. Also, having done the middle, you'll have a solid idea, of course, of what your paper is about. You'll know, for instance, which questions and answers are the most important. These may be different from the questions you asked before you did your research.

Now, then, you'll be able to write the introduction with some confidence. An example might be the following:

> A common image many people have of college athletes is that they are "dumb jocks." That is, they may be good on the playing field but not in the classroom. Is this true? The data vary for different sports, colleges, class levels, and other factors. This paper examines these differences.

Write the End. Finally, you write *III. End.* The end is the conclusion. It does not introduce any new facts or examples. It provides just the general answer or answers to the main question or questions raised in the beginning. This is the answer you've arrived at by exploring the questions in the middle section. It's possible, of course, that your conclusion will be incomplete or tentative. It's all right to state that further research is needed.

An example of the end of a paper might be as follows:

> As we have seen, although the dropout rate is higher for players in some sports and in some schools, it is not in others. Moreover, college athletes often graduate with honors, and some go on not only to professional sports but also to Rhodes scholarships, Fulbright and Wilson fellowships, and graduate and professional schools. Today the "strong-back, weak-brain" athlete of the past is largely a myth.

SOME WRITING TIPS   In writing the first draft of the middle, or body, of the paper, you should try to get something down that you can revise and polish later. Thus, don't worry too much if this initial version seems choppy; that's why a first draft is called a "rough" draft.

As you write, try to follow these guidelines:

Make Your Point and Give Support. The point you want to make is the answer to each question. (For example, your question might be "Does football require more intelligence than other major sports?") In your writing, this answer will become a statement. *Example:*

> It's possible that football requires greater intelligence than other major sports do.

Then support the statement with evidence, data, statistics, examples, and quotations. *Example:*

> Memorizing and executing scores or hundreds of different plays, for instance, takes a lot of intelligence. When scouts for pro football teams look over college players, one question they ask is, "How is he at learning the playbook?" [Then footnote the source.]

Quote Experts. It makes your statements or arguments much more convincing when you can buttress them with brief quotes from experts. Quoting authorities also can make your paper much more interesting and readable to the instructor. One caution, however: Don't overdo it with the quotations. Keep them brief.

You can also *paraphrase* experts—restate what they said, using your own words—to give variety to your writing.

Note: In either case, always credit your source!

Avoid Irrelevancies. Don't think you have to use all your research. That is, don't feel you have to try to impress your instructor by showing how much work you've done in your investigation. Just say what you need to say. Avoid piling on lots of irrelevant information, which will only distract and irritate your reader.

Give the Source of Your Data and Examples. Your instructor will want to know where you got your supporting information. Thus, be sure to provide sources. These can be expressed with precision on the final draft, following the particular footnote and bibliography ("works cited") style you've decided on. For now put some sort of shorthand for your sources in the first draft.

For instance, at the end of the sentence about the football playbook, you could provide the author and page for the source in parentheses. *Example:* ". . . learning the playbook?' (Wahlstrom 2002, p. 23)."

Jot Down Ideas. As you proceed through the first draft, jot down any ideas that come to you that don't immediately seem to fit anywhere. You may find a place for them later.

Take Breaks. Professional writers find that physical activity gives the mind a rest and triggers new ideas. The brain needs to disengage. Take short breaks to relax. Go get a soda, stroll down the corridor, take a walk outside, or otherwise move your body a bit. Take pen and paper and jot down thoughts.

LET THE DRAFT SIT   Many students write papers right up against their deadlines. It's far, far better, however, if you can get the first draft done early and let it sit in a drawer for a day or so. This will allow you to come back and revise it with a fresh perspective.

THE PRESENTATION: DO YOUR PAPER ON A WORD PROCESSOR OR TYPEWRITER   Presentation is important. Some instructors accept handwritten papers, but they'd rather not, because they're harder to read. In a job interview situation, you have to sell yourself not only with your experience, but also by the way you dress and present yourself. Similarly, you have to sell your paper not only by its ideas, but also by its presentation. In a distance learning course, you may be required to submit your paper to your instructor as an e-mail attachment.

Thus, the ideal choice is to type your paper on a word processor. You need not be expert; using two fingers instead of ten just means typing will take a little longer. You can type (keyboard) on the machine, print out a draft, and make corrections on the draft with a pencil. Then you can type in the corrections and print out a clean draft. Don't forget to give the paper a title page, including your name.

Phase 5: Revising, Finalizing, & Proofreading Your Paper

How much time should revising take? One suggestion is this: Phases 1–4 should take half your time, and Phase 5 should take the other half of your time. This rule shows the importance of revision.

The steps to take in revision are as follows:

- Read the paper aloud or get someone else to read it.
- Delete irrelevant material.
- Write transitions and do any reorganizing.
- Do fine-tuning and polishing.
- Type the paper.
- Proofread the paper.
- Make a copy.

READ ALOUD OR HAVE SOMEONE ELSE READ DRAFTS OF YOUR PAPER   It's hard to spot our own mistakes, particularly during a silent reading. To better catch these, try the following:

- ***Read your draft aloud to yourself.*** If you read aloud what you've written, whether first draft or revised draft, you'll be able to spot missing words, awkward usage, and missing details.
- ***Get feedback from another person.*** By having a friend, family member, or the instructor read any of your drafts, you can get the help of an "editor." (You can offer to read friends' papers in exchange.) Any additional feedback can be valuable.

    Special Note: Don't take the criticism personally. If your readers say your paper is "illogical" or "vague," they are not implying you're stupid. When people criticize your draft, they are not criticizing you as a human being. Moreover, remember you don't *have* to do what they say. You're looking for suggestions, not commandments.

DELETE IRRELEVANT MATERIAL   The best way to start the revision is to take a pencil and start crossing out words. Like a film maker cutting scenes so a movie won't run too long and bore the audience, you should cut your paper to its essentials.

This is what editors call "blue penciling." Strive for conciseness and brevity. As a mental guideline, imagine someone writing "Repetitious!" or "Redundant!" or

"Wordy!" in the margin. Be ruthless. First cut unnecessary sections, pages, and paragraphs. Then cut unnecessary sentences, phrases, and words. Cut even your best ideas and phrases—those gems you're proud of—if they don't move the essay along and advance your case.

WRITE TRANSITIONS AND DO ANY REORGANIZING   You may have written the first draft fairly rapidly and not given much thought to making transitions—logical connections—between thoughts. You may also have deleted such connections when you blue-penciled material above. Now's the time to make sure the reader is able to move logically from one of your ideas to another.

You may well discover while doing this that your paper needs to be reorganized, that your outline isn't working right. You can use the "cut-and-paste" function in your word processing program to move things around. Or, if you like a more hands-on, "big-picture" approach, you can print out your draft and then use scissors and tape to resequence major paragraphs.

DO FINE-TUNING AND POLISHING   Now you need to take a pencil and do a final edit to make sure everything reads well.

Some suggestions:

- *Have a thesis statement.* Make sure the introduction to the paper has a thesis statement that says what the main point of your paper is.
- *Guide the reader.* Tell the reader what you're going to do. Introduce each change in topic. Connect topics by writing transitions.
- *Present supporting data.* Make sure you have enough examples, quotations, and data to support your assertions.
- *Don't be wordy.* Don't be infatuated with the exuberance and prolixity of your own verbosity. Don't use big words when short ones will do. Delete unnecessary words.
- *Check grammar and spelling.* Check your paper for grammatical mistakes. Also check for spelling. Look up words you're not sure about.
- *Follow correct style for documentation.* Follow the instructor's directions, if any, for documenting your sources. The humanities, for example, follow the style developed by the Modern Language Association (MLA). The social sciences follow the style developed by the American Psychological Association (APA). Guidebooks are available in the campus bookstore or at the library.

  A popular style (MLA) is to identify the author's last name and the page reference within parentheses. For example:

  > As one <u>New York Times</u> reporter summarized the NCAA study, white male athletes and nonathletes graduated at the same rate. But athletes had a better graduation rate than nonathletes among black women, black men, and white women (Litsky C19).

  You then present a complete description of each source in an alphabetical listing at the end of the paper entitled "Works Cited." For example:

Works Cited

Bradley, Bill. *Values of the Game.* New York: Broadway Books, 1998.

Litsky, Frank. "Athletes' Graduation Rate Surpasses Nonathletes'." *New York Times* 27 June 1997, C19.

Suggs, Welch. "Fight Over NCAA Standards Reflects Long-Standing Dilemma." *The Chronicle of Higher Education* 9 April 2000, A48.

PROOFREAD   Have you had past papers come back from the instructor with red ink circling spelling and grammatical mistakes? Those red circles probably negatively affected your final grade, marking you down from, say, an A– to a B+.

With your paper in beautiful, final, typed form (and the hand-in deadline perhaps only hours away), you may be tempted not to proofread it. You may not only be supremely tired of the whole thing but not want to "mess it up" by making handwritten corrections. *Do it anyway.* The instructor won't have any excuse then to give you red circles for small mistakes. And if you're using a word processor, providing a completely clean final draft is very easy.

MAKE A COPY   Papers do get lost or stolen after they've been handed in (or on a student's way to handing it in). If you typed your paper on a word processor, make sure you save a copy on a floppy disk. Otherwise, use a photocopying machine at the library or an instant-printing shop to make a copy.

Notes

Chapter 2

1. Study by Impulse for *Iconoclast* newsletter. Reported in Plotnikoff, D. E. (1999, April 4). E-mail: A critical medium has reached critical mass. *San Jose Mercury News,* pp. 1F, 2F.

2. Adapted from Elizabeth Weise, Successful net search starts with need, *USA Today,* January 24, 2000, p. 3D; and other sources.

3. Matt Lake, M. (1993, September 3). Desperately seeking Susan or Suzie NOT Sushi. *New York Times,* p. D1.

4. Morris, K. M. *User's guide to the information age.* New York: Lightbulb Press, 1999, pp. 111, 153.

Chapter 3

1. Myers, D. G. (1992). *The pursuit of happiness: Who is happy—and why.* New York: William Morrow.

2. Samuelson, R. J. (1996, July 1). The endless road "crisis." *Newsweek,* p. 47.

3. Robinson, J. P., & Godbey, G. (1997). *Time for life.* University Park, PA: Penn State University Press. Quoted in Hirsch, A. (1997, July 26). Author says there's more free time than we think. *San Francisco Chronicle,* p. A21; reprinted from *Baltimore Sun.*

4. Beneke, W. M., & Harris, M. B. (1972). Teaching self-control of study behavior. *Behavior Research* & *Therapy,* pp. 10, 35–41.

5. Kessinger, T. G. Quoted in Marriott, M. (1991, April 12). In high-tech dorms, a call for power. *New York Times,* pp. A1, A8.

6. Anonymous (2000, June 22). Web crawlers don't surf alone. *USA Today,* p. 1A.

7. Puente, M. (2000, April 25). Multi-tasking to the max. *USA Today,* pp. 1D, 1E.

8. Wen, P. (2000, May 27). Expert advice for those who try two things at once—"chill out." *San Francisco Chronicle,* p. A10.

9. Pollar, O. (1998, August 3). How to avoid the overload of information. *San Francisco Examiner,* p. J-3.

10. Ellis, D. (1991). *Becoming a master student* (6th ed.). Rapid City, SD: College Survival, Inc., p. 53.

11. Lakein, A. (1973). *How to get control of your time and your life.* New York: Peter H. Wyden.

12. Sapadin, L. (1997). *It's about time.* New York: Penguin.

13. Sapadin, L. Reported in Peterson, K. S. (1997, July 22). Helping procrastinators get to it. *USA Today,* p. 7D.

14. Zimbardo, P. G. (1977). *Shyness: What it is, what to do about it.* Reading, MA: Addison-Wesley, p. 14.

15. Robinson & Godbey, 1997. See note 3.

16. Haron, D. (1994, June 23). Campus drinking problem becomes severe [letter]. *New York Times,* p. A14.

17. Hanson, D. J. (1994, September 28). Parents: Don't panic about campus boozers [letter]. *New York Times,* p. A11.

18. Wechsler, H., et al. (1994, December 7). Health and behavioral consequences of binge drinking in college. *Journal of the American Medical Association.*

19. Associated Press (1992, September 20). Study finds more drinking at small colleges than large ones. *New York Times,* sec. 1, p. 20.

20. della Cava, M. R. (1996, January 16). Are heavy users hooked or just on-line fanatics? *USA Today,* pp. 1A, 2A.

21. Howe, K. (1995, April 5). Diary of an AOL addict. *San Francisco Chronicle,* pp. Dl, D3; and Hamilton, K., & Kalb, C. (1995, December 18). They log on, but they can't log off. *Newsweek,* pp. 60–61.

22. Yu, S., quoted in Hamilton & Kalb, 1995. See note 22.

23. Kandell, J. J., quoted in Young, J. R. (1998, February 6). Students are unusually vulnerable to Internet addiction, article says. *Chronicle of Higher Education,* p. A25.

24. American Psychological Association, reported in Leibrock, R. (1997, October 22). AOL-aholic: Tales of an online addict. *Reno News & Review,* pp. 21, 24.

25. Hamilton & Kalb, 1995. See note 22.

26. Sanchez, R. (1996, May 23). Colleges seek ways to reach Internet-addicted students. *San Francisco Chronicle,* p. A16; reprinted from *Washington Post.*

27. Sanchez, 1996. See note 227.

28. Belluck, P. (1996, December 1). The symptoms of Internet addiction. *New York Times,* sec. 4, p. 5.

29. Jacoby, B. (1989). The student-as-commuter: Developing a comprehensive institutional response. *Ashe-Eric Higher Education Report 7.* In Stewart, S. S., & Rue, P. (1983). Commuter students: Definition and distribution. In Stewart, S. S. (Ed.). *Commuter students: Enhancing their educational experiences.* San Francisco: Jossey-Bass; and Wright, S. E. (1996, October 13). Is there any hope for Silicon Valley's worst commute? *San Jose Mercury News,* pp. 1P, 3P.

30. Castaneda, C. J., & Sham, L. (1996, August 16). Car pools: Too much time and trouble for a lot of riders. *USA Today,* p. 8A.

31. Hamilton, E. (1996, August 8). When should a teen get a car? *Point Reyes Light,* p. 6.

32. Tyson, E. (1996, August 18). Kicking the car habit. *San Francisco Examiner,* pp. D-l, D-2.

33. King, J. E. (1998, May 1). Too many students are holding jobs for too many hours. *Chronicle of Higher Education,* p. A72.

34. Research by U.S. Department of Education, National Center for Education Statistics, reported in King, 1998. See note 33.

35. King, 1998. See note 33.

36. U.S. Department of Education, *1995–96 National Postsecondary Student Aid Study,* reported in King, 1998. See note 35.

37. King, 1998. See note 33.

Chapter 4

1. Cited in Ducharme, A., & Watford, L., *Explanation of assessment areas* [handout].

2. Bloom, B. S., Englehart, M. D., Furst, E. J., & Krathwohl, D. R. (1965). *Taxonomy of educational objectives: Cognitive domain.* New York: David McKay.

3. Gordon, B., quoted in Yoffe, E. (1997, October 13). How quickly we forget. *U.S. News & World Report,* pp. 53–57.

4. Lapp, D. C. (1992, December). (Nearly) total recall. *Stanford Magazine,* pp. 48–51.

5. Ebbinghaus, H. (1913). *Memory.* New York: Teachers College. (Original work published 1885.)

6. Survey by National Institute for Development and Administration, University of Texas. Cited in Lapp, 1992. See note 4.

7. Pauk, W. (1989). *How to study in college* (4th ed.). Boston: Houghton-Miffiin, p. 92.

8. Pauk, 1989, p. 92. See note 7.

9. Krueger, W. C. F. (1929). The effect of overlearning on retention. *Journal of Experimental Psychology,* pp. 12, 71–78.

10. Weiten, W., Lloyd, M. A., & Lashley, R. L. (1990). *Psychology applied to modern life: Adjustment in the 90s* (3rd ed.). Pacific Grove, CA: Brooks/Cole.

11. Bromage, B. K., & Mayer, R. E. (1986). Quantitative and qualitative effects of repetition on learning from technical text. *Journal of Educational Psychology,* 78(4), pp. 271–78.

12. Zechmeister, E. B., & Nyberg, S. E. (1982). *Human memory: An introduction to research and theory.* Pacific Grove, CA: Brooks/Cole.

13. Kalat, J. W. (1990). *Introduction to psychology* (2nd ed.). Belmont, CA: Wadsworth, p. 295.

14. Doner, K. (1994, March). Improve your memory. *American Health,* pp. 56–60.

15. Underwood, B. J. (1957). Interference and forgetting. *Psychological Review,* pp. 64, 49–60.

16. Fowler, M. J., Sullivan, M. J., & Ekstrand, B. R. (1973). Sleep and memory. *Science,* pp. 179, 302–304.

17. Thorndyke, P. W., & Hayes-Roth, B. (1979). The use of schemata in the acquisition and transfer of knowledge. *Cognitive Psychology,* 11, pp. 83–106.

18. Craik, F. I. M., & Lockhart, R. S. (1972). Levels of processing: A framework for memory research. *Journal of Verbal Learning & Verbal Behavior,* pp. 11, 671–84.

19. Raugh, M. R., & Atkinson, R. C. (1975). A mnemonic method for learning a second-language vocabulary. *Journal of Educational Psychology,* pp. 67, 1–16.

20. Intons-Peterson, M. J., & Fournier, J. (1986). External and internal memory aids: When and how often do we use them? *Journal of Experimental Psychology: General,* pp. 116, 267–80.

21. Bower, G. H. (1970). Organizational factors in memory. *Cognitive Psychology,* pp. 1, 18–46.

22. Doner, 1994. See note 14.

23. Bower, G. H., & Clark, M. C. (1969). Narrative stories as mediators of serial learning. *Psychonomic Science,* pp. 14, 181–82.

24. Weiten, W., Lloyd, M. A., & Lashley, R. L. (1990). *Psychology applied to modern life: Adjustment in the 90s* (3rd ed.). Pacific Grove, CA: Brooks/Cole, p. 24. Adapted from Bower & Clark, 1969. See note 23.

25. Robinson, F. P. (1970). *Effective study* (4th ed.). New York. Harper & Row.

26. Pauk, W. (1989). *How to study in college* (4th ed.). Boston: Houghton Mifflin, p. 181.

27. Pauk, 1989, p. 122. See note 26.

28. Walter, T., & Siebert, A. (1990). *Student success* (5th ed.). Fort Worth, TX: Holt, Rinehart and Winston, pp. 96–97.

29. Walter & Siebert, 1990. See note 28.

30. Starke, M. C. (1993). *Strategies for college success* (2nd ed.). Englewood Cliffs, NJ: Prentice Hall, p. 82.

Chapter 5

1. Walter, T., & Siebert, A. (1990). *Student success: How to succeed in college and still have time for your friends.* Fort Worth, TX: Holt, Rinehart and Winston, pp. 108–109.

2. Walter & Siebert, 1990, p. 103. See note 1.

3. Borgman, C. quoted in Chapman, G. (1995, August 21). What the online world really needs is an old-fashioned librarian. *San Jose Mercury News,* p. 3D; reprinted from *Los Angeles Times.*

Index

114